❧ THE WRITERS ❧

THE WRITERS
A Sense of Ireland

New work by 44 Irish writers selected and edited by

ANDREW CARPENTER

and

PETER FALLON

with photographs of the writers by

MIKE BUNN

GEORGE BRAZILLER

NEW YORK

First published 1980 by the O'Brien Press Dublin
and in United States of America by
George Braziller Inc., One Park Avenue
New York, N.Y. 10016

For information address the publisher:
George Braziller, Inc.
One Park Avenue
New York, N.Y. 10016

Library of Congress Cataloging in Publication Data

The Writers.

   Bibliography: p.
   Includes index.
   1. Irish literature – 20th century. Irish literature –
20th century –Translations into English. 3. English
literature – Irish authors. 4. English literature –
20th century. 5. English literature – Translations from
Irish. I. Carpenter, Andrew. II. Fallon, Peter, 1951 –
PB1427.W7   820'.8'09415   80–12681

ISBN 0–8076–0970–6

Jacket and book design JARLATH HAYES
Typesetting DESIGN & ART FACILITIES, DUBLIN
Printing A FOLENS & CO LTD, DUBLIN
Binding JOHN F NEWMAN, DUBLIN

Chance and Destiny have between them woven two-thirds of all history, and of the history of Ireland wellnigh the whole. The literature of a nation, on the other hand, is spun out of its heart. If you would know Ireland – body and soul – you must read its poems and stories. They came into existence to please nobody but the people of Ireland. Government did not make them on the one hand, nor bad seasons on the other. They are Ireland talking to herself.

W. B. YEATS

CONTENTS

ACKNOWLEDGEMENTS

The epigraph, taken from W. B. Yeats's introduction to *Representative Irish Tales* (1891) is reprinted by kind permission of Mr. Michael Yeats and Miss Anne Yeats. *Representative Irish Tales* was re-issued by Colin Smythe Limited in 1979.

The passage from Samuel Beckett's forthcoming new novel *Company* was made available by John Calder to whom we express our thanks. *Company* is to appear from John Calder (Publishers) in May 1980.

A version of Part III of Seamus Heaney's "Sweeney Astray" originally appeared in *The New Yorker*.

We thank Seamus Cashman of Wolfhound Press for providing Liam O'Flaherty's unfinished story.

The original Irish poems from which Seán Ó Tuama has provided the translations printed here are included in his recent collection *Saol Fó Thoinn*.

The photographs of Aidan Higgins, Jennifer Johnston and James Simmons were not taken by Mike Bunn. Those of Aidan Higgins and Jennifer Johnston were provided by the authors and that of James Simmons, which was taken by Don McPhee, appears by courtesy of Blackstaff Press.

The props used in Mike Bunn's image of Samuel Beckett were provided by The Abbey Theatre, and our thanks are due to Deirdre McQuillan for her help. We should also like to thank Seamus Cashman, Seamus Deane, Susan and Jarlath Hayes, Jim McGivern, Philippa Kidd, Michael O'Brien, Sheila O'Higgins, John Stephenson, Kitty Tailer, Alice Watson, David Collins, Michael Longley, and Messrs Arthur Guinness. Particular thanks are also due to Ann Rigney who compiled and wrote the biographical notes which appear at the end of the book.

The publisher gratefully acknowledges the assistance of An Chomhairle Ealaíon and The Arts Council of Northern Ireland.

INTRODUCTION

After ten years of upheaval – not only the 'Troubles' in the north of Ireland but also fundamental political and social changes in the south – Irish writing is healthier, more vital, more searching than it has been for fifty years. The writers included in this book range in age from under 25 to over 80 and differ widely in their choice of subject matter and theme. But they all share at least two characteristics – whether they write plays, prose or poetry, in Irish or in English – a concern with the craft of writing and a vision qualified in a subtle yet persuasive way by an Irish perspective. There is a sense of irony, of self-mockery almost, in much writing in this book which suggests that Irish writers are as interested in self-definition as in any external subject. Uncertainties force the writer in upon himself and the result, in this book at any rate, seems to be a controlled but intense vision of man and his environment.

All the writers in this book are Irish in a broad sense. The majority live in Ireland and were born here: some who were born here live elsewhere, but have retained strong links with Ireland. For some, Ireland is home if not motherland. For all, however, Irish culture and perspective is of controlling importance.

It was a desire to focus attention on Irish culture in general which led, indirectly, to this book as all those whose work appears here were originally invited to take part in 'A Sense of Ireland', a festival of Irish arts in London in the spring of 1980. Some of those who contribute to the bookwere not, in fact, able to read at the festival: some who were able to take part in the festival were not able to provide new material in time for us to include it in the book. Among those whom we asked to contribute but who were unable to were Brian Coffey, John McGahern, Derek Mahon, Michael McLaverty, Máire Mhac an tSaoi, Brian Moore, Edna O'Brien and Máirtín O Direáin.

The book is arranged so that a photograph of the writer faces the first page of his or her work. These photographs, taken especially by Mike Bunn, provide a striking exploration in themselves of the personalities of those writing in Ireland today.

We are grateful to all those whose work appears here for providing us with new or unpublished material. Without them, the book . . . .

ANDREW CARPENTER
PETER FALLON

from

Kepler

a novel

AT DUSK HE RODE OUT of the forest of Schönbuch. The bright March day had turned to storm, and a brooding tawny light was sinking in the valley. The Neckar glimmered, slate-blue and cold. He stopped on the brow of the hill and stood in the stirrups to breathe deep the brave tempestuous air. He remembered Swabia not like this, strange and fierce; was it he, perhaps, who had changed? He had new gloves, twenty florins in his purse, leave of absence from the Stiftsschule, this dappled grey mare lent him by his friend the district secretary Stefan Speidel, and, safe in a satchel by his side, wrapped in oilskin, most precious of all, his manuscript. The book was done, and he had come to Tübingen to publish it. Black rain was falling when he entered the narrow streets of the town, and lanterns flickered on the bastioned walls of Hohentübingen high above him. After the July revelation it had taken seven more weary months of labour, and the incorporation of a third dimension into his calculations, to round out the theory and complete the *Mysterium*. Night, storm, a solitary traveller, the muted magnificence of the world; a trickle of rain got under his collar, and his shoulder-blades quivered, as if remembering a pre-natal empyrean.

Presently he was sitting in bed in a low brown room at The Boar, a filthy blanket pulled to his chin, eating oatcakes and drinking mulled wine. Rain drummed on the roof. From the tavern below there rose a raucous singing – fine hearty people, the Swabians, and prodigious topers. Many a skinful of Rhenish he himself as a student had puked up on that rush-strewn floor down there. It surprised him, how happy he was to be home. He was downing the dregs of the jug in a final toast to Mistress Fame, that large and jaunty goddess, when the potboy banged on the door and summoned him forth. Bleared and grinning, half drunk, and still with the blanket clutched about him, he struggled down the rickety stairs. The aleroom had the look of a ship's cabin, the drinkers swaying, candlelight swinging, and, beyond the streaming windows, the heaving of the oceanic night. Michael Mästlin rose from a table in the inglenook. They shook hands, and found themselves grappling with an unexpected shyness. Johannes without preamble said: "I have written my book," and frowned at the filthy table and the leathern cups: why did things not quake at that announcement? "I have *finished* it, the *Mysterium*," his voice breaking.

Professor Mästlin was eyeing the blanket. "Are you ill?"

"What? No; cold, wet. I have lately arrived. You had my message? But of course, since you are . . . here. Though my piles, forgive my mentioning it, are terrible, after that journey."

"You don't mean to lodge here, surely? – no, no, you shall stay with me. Come, lean on my arm, we must see to your bags."

"I am not – "

"Come now, I say; you are on fire, man, and your hands, look, they're shaking."

"I am not, I tell you, I am *not ill*."

The fever lasted for three days. He was convinced he would die. Supine on a couch in Mästlin's rooms he was plagued by visions of gaudy devastation and travail. He raved and prayed, clawing at his slimed hair. His flesh oozed a noxious sweat: where did it come from, so much poison? Mästlin nursed him with a bachelor's unhandly tenderness, and one morning he awoke, a delicate vessel lined with glass, and saw through an angle of window above him small clouds sailing in a patch of blue sky, and he was well.

He had passed through a refining fire, his brain rinsed clear by the flames of the fever. Squatting in a tangle of sheets he attacked his manuscript, scoring and cutting and splicing, taking the theory apart and reassembling it plane by plane until it seemed to him miraculous in its newfound elegance and strength. The window above him boomed, buffeted by the gale. He imagined washes of that eminent exhilarated air sweeping through him also. Mästlin brought him his food, boiled fish, soups, stewed lights, but otherwise left him alone now; he was nervous of this excitable phenomenon, twenty years his junior, perched there on the couch in a soiled nightshirt, like an animated doll, day after day, scribbling. He warned that the sickness was not gone, that it had only entered another phase. Johannes agreed, for what was this rage, this rapture, if not an ailment of a kind?

But he recovered from it. At the end of a week the old doubts and fears were back. He turned to Mästlin for reassurance. The Professor, shying under this intensity of need, frowned into a middle distance, as if surreptitiously spying out a hole down which to bolt. "Yes," he said, coughing, "yes, the idea is, ah, ingenious, certainly."

"But do you think it is *true?*"

Mästlin's frown deepened. It was a Sunday morning. They walked on the common behind the main hall of the university. The elms thrashed under a violent sky. The Professor had a grizzled beard and a drinker's nose. He weighed matters carefully before committing them to words. Europe considered him a great astronomer. *True?* – what in God's name did he mean, true? "I am," he announced, "of the opinion that the mathematician has achieved his goal when he advances hypotheses to which the phenomena correspond as closely as possible; you yourself would also withdraw, I believe, if someone could offer still better principles than yours. It by no means follows that the reality immediately conforms to the detailed hypotheses of every master."

Johannes, debilitated and ill-tempered, scowled. This was the first time he had ventured out since the fever had abated. He felt transparent. There was a whirring high in the air, and then suddenly a crash of bells that made his very bones vibrate. "Why waste words?" he said, yelled, bells, *damn* – "geometry existed before the Creation, is co-eternal with the mind of God, *is God himself . . .*"

"O!"

". . . For what," smoothly, "exists in God that is not God himself?" A grey wind swarmed through the grass to meet him; he shivered. "But we are mouthing quotations merely: tell me what you truly think."

"I have said what I think," Mästlin snapped.

"But that, forgive me, magister, is scholastic shilly-shally."

"Well then, I am a schoolman!"

"You? who teaches his students – who taught *me* – the helio-centric doctrine of Copernicus, *you* a schoolman?" but turned on the Professor all the same a side-long speculative glance.

Mästlin pounced. "Aha, but that was also a school-man, *and* a saver of the phenomena!"

"He only – "

"A schoolman, sir! Copernicus respected the ancients."

"Well then; but I do not?"

"It seems to me, young man, that you have not much respect for anything!"

"I respect the past," Johannes said mildly. "But I wonder if it is the business of scientists to follow slavishly the teaching of former masters?"

He did: he wondered: was it? Raindrops like conjured coins spattered the paved pathway. They gained the porch of the Aula Maxima. The doors were shut and bolted within, but there was space enough for them to shelter under the stone Platonic seal. They stood in silence, gazing out. Mästlin breathed heavily, his annoyance working him like a bellows. Johannes, oblivious, idly noted a flock of sheep upon the common, their lugubriously noble heads, their calm eyes, how they champed the grass with such fastidiousness, as if they were not merely feeding, but performing a delicate and onerous labour; God's mute meaningless creatures, so many and various. Sometimes like this the world bore in upon him suddenly, all that which is without apparent pattern or shape, but simply *there.* The wind tossed a handful of rooks out of the great trees. Faintly there came the sound of singing, and up over the slope of the common a ragged file of young boys marched, wading against the gale. Their song, one of Luther's stolid hymns, quavered in the tumultuous air. Kepler with a pang recognised the shapeless tunic of the seminary: thus he, once. They passed by, a tenfold ghost, and, as the rain grew heavier, broke file and scampered the last few paces, yelling, into the shelter of St. Anne's chapel under the elms. Mästlin was saying: ". . . to Stuttgart, where I have business at Duke Frederick's court." He paused, waiting in vain for a response; his tone was conciliatory. "I have drawn up a calendar at the Duke's bidding, and must deliver it . . ." He tried again, with a renewed angry edge: "You have done similar work, of course."

"What? O, calendars, yes; it is all a necromantic monkeyshine though."

Mästlin stared. "All . . . ?"

"Sortilege and star magic, all that. And yet," pausing, "I believe that the stars do influence our affairs. It's curious . . ." He broke off and frowned; the past was marching through his head into a limitless future.

Heard in the Dark

an extract from COMPANY *a novel*

THE LAST TIME YOU WENT OUT the snow lay on the ground. You now lying in the dark stand that morning on the sill having pulled the door gently to behind you. You lean back against the door with bowed head making ready to set out. By the time you open your eyes your feet have disappeared and the skirts of your greatcoat come to rest on the surface of the snow. The dark scene seems lit from below. You see yourself at that last outset leaning against the door with closed eyes waiting for the word from you to go. You? To be gone. Then the snowlit scene. You lie in the dark with closed eyes and see yourself there as described making ready to strike out and away across the expanse of light. You hear again the click of the door pulled gently to and the silence before the steps can start. Next thing you are on your way across the white pasture afrolic with lambs in spring and strewn with red placentae. You take the course you always take which is a beeline for the gap or ragged point in the quickset that forms the western fringe. Thither from your entering the pasture you need normally from eighteen hundred to two thousand paces depending on your humour and the state of the ground. But on this last morning many more will be necessary. Many many more. The beeline is so familiar to your feet that if necessary they could keep to it and you sightless with error on arrival of not more than a few feet north or south. And indeed without any such necessity unless from within this is what they normally do and not only here. For you advance if not with closed eyes though this as often as not at least with them fixed on the momentary ground before your feet. That is all of nature you have seen. Since you finally bowed your head. The fleeting ground before your feet. From time to time. You do not count your steps any more. For the simple reason they number each day the same. Average day in day out the same. The way being always the same. You keep count of the days and every tenth night multiply. And add. Your father's shade is not with you any more. It fell out long ago. You do not hear your footfalls any more. Unhearing unseeing you go your way. Day after day. The same way. As if there were no other any more. For you there is no other any more. You used never to halt except to make your reckoning. So as to plod on from nought anew. This need removed as we have seen there is none in theory to halt any more. Save perhaps a moment at the outermost point. To gather yourself together for the return. And yet you do. As never before. Not for tiredness. You are no more tired now than you always were. Not because of age. You are no older now than you always were. And yet you halt as never before. So that the same hundred yards you used to cover in a matter of three to four minutes may now take you anything from fifteen to twenty. The foot falls unbidden in midstep or next for lift cleaves to the ground bringing the body to a stand. Then a speechlessness whereof the gist. Can they go on? Or better, Shall they go on? The barest gist. Stilled when finally as always hitherto they do. You lie in the dark with closed eyes and see the scene. As you could not at the time. The dark cope of sky. The dazzling land. You at a standstill in the midst. The quarterboots sunk to the tops. The skirts of the greatcoat resting on the snow. In the old bowed head in the old block hat speechless misgiving. Halfway across the pasture on your beeline to the gap. The unerring feet fast. You look behind you as you could not then and see their trail. A great swerve. Withershins. Almost as if all at once the heart too heavy. In the end too heavy.

The Ballad
of Beauty and Time

Plainly came the time
  The eucalyptus tree
Could not succour me
Nor the honey pot,
The sunshine vitamin,
Nor even getting thin.
I had passed my prime.

Then when bagged ash,
Scalded quarts of water,
Oil of the lime,
Cinders for the skin
And honey all had failed,
I sorted out my money
And went to buy some time.

I knew the right address:
The occult house of shame
Where all the women came
Shopping for a mouth,
A new nose, an eyebrow
And entered without knocking
And stood as I did now.

A shape with a knife
Stooped away from me
Cutting something vague.
It might have been a face.
I couldn't really see.
I coughed once and said
"I need a lease of life".

The room was full of masks,
Lines of grins gaping,
A wall of skin stretching,
A chin he had re-worked,
A face he had re-made.
He slit and tucked and cut,
Then straightened from his blade.

"A tuck, a hem," he said,
"I only seam the line,
I only mend the dress.
I wouldn't do for you.
Your quarrel's with the weave.
The best I achieve
Is just a stitch in time."

I started out again.
I knew a studio
Full of chiselled heels
Strewn in marble shock.
I saw the sculptor there
Soldering a nose
And button-holed his smock:

"It's all very well.
When you have bronzed a woman,
Pinioned her and finned
Wings on either shoulder
Anyone can see
She won't get any older.
What's that to do with me?

"See the last of youth
Slumming in my skin,
My sham pink mouth.
Here behold your critic,

The threat to your aesthetic:
I am the brute proof
Beauty is not truth."

"Truth is in our lies"
The good old man replied.
"This woman fledged in stone,
The centre of all eyes,
Her own museum-blind,
We sharpen with our skills
The arts of compromise.

And all I have cast
In crystal or in glass
In lapis or in onyx
Is from my knowledge of
When from the honest flaw
To lift and stay my hand
And say 'Let it stand'."

Four poems from

The Rose Geranium

III

I run my hand along the clean wood
And at once I am stroking the heads
Of everyone in the room.
                  Looking into the grain
Wavered and kinked like hairlines, what I see
Is the long currents of a pale ocean
Softly turning itself inside out.

Palm slack as air's belly touching the sea –
I feel the muscles tugging
In the wood, shoals hauling.

I look in vain for that boat
Biting its groove to the south-east,
For that storm, the knot of blindness
That left us thrashing
In steel corridors in the dark.

Beyond the open window
Along the silkpacked alleys of the souq
Momentary fountains and stairways
      (My hands move over the table
        Feeling the spines of fish and the keels)
I look, and fail, in the street
Searching for a man with hair like yours.

IV

Alone I walk in a wood above Holyoke:
The white birch faces me, a peeled dead look,
Moonlit matt affronting the morning.

My skin is growing again, in air
Warm like a quilt. The trees
Are as close as a friend and a bottle.

Roadside gravel displays floodwater marks
And a scatter of wrappers thrown from cars.
Girdled with rust a white stone
Is disclosed among the husks, washed clean.

In the sky a pod full of people
Roars east to Boston.

V

AMELIA

Remembering her half-sister Amelia, that girl
Whose hips askew made every step seem upstairs
The girl at the airport tells me that from her
One spring she bought the first small car.

After that it was trains and taxis for Amelia
For years and years, while the younger lay
In the car in a leafy mews in Dublin
Making love to a bald actor
Her elbow tightening
Linked through the steering-wheel.

She tells me, this hot noisy afternoon,
That Amelia now drives a car like a cabin-cruiser
In Halifax, Nova Scotia, where her husband
Fishes for lobster in short ice-free summers.

VI

So rarely we lie
As then, in darkness
A vertical gleam relieved
Where the brilliance from outside
Struck the glass over the hearth

– Breast high, if one stood,
Night lapped the bookshelves
And a dying light floated
Above us, never reaching
Us, our arrested embrace

– I think at once of
That amphibious
Twilight, now that the year is
Revisiting the spring shrine.
From my window the cold, grey

Rectangles of stone –
February light
Spreading across the walls over my head
Washes my room with shadows, cold until morning.

Christmas at Beaconsfield

an excerpt from a long poem

(Edmund Burke has invited Sir James Mackintosh down to Beacons-field to spend Christmas 1796 with him. Mackintosh, famous then as the author of a tract supporting the French Revolution, is about to be converted by Burke to an hostility towards the Revolution and all it represents. His career is about to be blighted. It is snowing outside.)

Beaconsfield. The snottish son dead.
Europe awash. Ireland in her
Customary decline. Omens.
Illuminati glimmered in the dusk
Of German duchies. Madame Guillotine
Was bright and still. "If we cry,
Like children, for the moon,
Like children, we must cry on."

Across from him sat Mackintosh,
Warm with wine and with the glare
Of a great log fire. The ceiling
Was whitened by the reflex of the snow
Through the great window out of which
Harmonies of space and light
Flowed and curled into the mouldings
Of the frieze. Hauteur and domesticity
Lived together in this room
And in its owner—hardly owner—
For he was mortgaged to the hilt,
An Irish blade in a Whig scabbard.

He faced the Scotsman who wore a mild
And slightly rictus grin that spoke
Surprise that such a man as Burke could be
So broken by that Parisian brawl
By which the French had tried to emulate
What 'we' had done since 1688.

Imagining that conversion, many times,
I hear the brogue thicken and bellow
On the name Rousseau; felt the sibilance
Of his hate for the dark Genevan.
"The spawn of his disgustful amours",
"The great apostle of benevolence".
The hand beating upon the velvet
Padding of his chair-arm. His "Sir!"
Veering to a snarl, his long, laborious
Penetrating grief—dead son, dead King and Queen
Ghosting the dulled room. Twenty-three
Years before in the Rue Royale
Round Baron d'Holbach's table
The waspish literati had stopped him cold.
(Almost certainly there was Diderot
With his Cyril Cusack face, the unbuttoned
Prince of Philosophers; Chastellux and St. Lambert,
God knows who else to make his hair
Stand on end, more even than Voltaire).

Poor Mackintosh. Brought to a broody, fearful
Stare at the caving fire while Burke
Glowered at the litter of his life,
Cursed the French for what they had done
When he was too old to win and had no son
To do it for him. The frost of years
In his hair, the ice of conviction
Melting in his eyes, an old man
Whose dinner-gong of a voice
Was comic and ineffectual
To the boneheads of the Commons.
Mackintosh could not look
Near him. Out of God's bare rood
The foliage of power spread and greened.
But in Ireland's and England's pleasant
Lands Misrule was Lord; though Hastings

Brought to Book, the Dublin junta
Schooled rebels, Fox and Foxites fooled
The Whigs; Parisian orators, lawyers and friseurs
Auctioned history to the mob.
Mackintosh shuddered. A lawyer who had
Vindicated France. He felt like a son
Who had broken a father's heart.
Faint shadows in rosewood stirred.
Burke wept. The clock struck. Christmas blurred.

The Drimoleague Blues

Oh I know this mean town is not always mean
And I know that you do not always mean what you mean
And the meaning of meaning can both mean and not mean:
But I mean to say; I mean to say;
I've got the Drimoleague Blues, I've got the Drimoleague Blues,
I've got the Drimoleague Blues so bad I can't move:
Even if you were to plug in Drimoleague to every oil-well in Arabia—
I'd still have the Drimoleague Blues.

Oh this town is so mean that it's got its own mean
And that's to be as mean as green, as mean as green:
Shoot a girl dead and win yourself a bride,
Shoot a horse dead and win yourself a car:
Oh I've got the Drimoleague Blues, I've got the Drimoleague Blues,
I've got the Drimoleague Blues so bad I can't move:
Even if you were to plug in Drimoleague to every oil-well in Arabia—
I'd still have the Drimoleague Blues.

And so on right down to the end of the line
Mean with Mean will always rhyme
And Man with Man: Oh, where is the Woman
With the Plough, where is her Daughter with the Stars?
Oh I've got the Drimoleague Blues, I've got the Drimoleague Blues,
I've got the Drimoleague Blues so bad I can't move:
Even if you were to plug in Drimoleague to every oil-well in Arabia—
I'd still have the Drimoleague Blues.

Two poems

CATHOLICS

The man at the bar is cursing women,
he hates his wife and loves his mother,
and tells who'll hear of the whores
he's ridden. When they hadn't a woman
they improvised, himself and another,

behind the ballrooms of their need
they actualized their monstrous art
and in the dark they dreamt of Mary.
And maybe I'm as bad –
I've come for the loan of an ass and cart

and listen to deeds at the Parish Sports
that gorged a greed that knew no bounds,
'Sports is right! That woman's a mother
in England now.' And he escaped. He ran
with the hare and chased with the hounds.

I'm enjoying the stout and the others'
talk but he badgers me,
'We'll have a big night out, both of us,
we'll travel far and find a pair
and none will know, there'll be nobody

the wiser.' And I say 'Aye'
and turn the talk to the ass's age,
her use for foddering, and mention
rain and local news – a death, a sale,
a harvest saved – but he's me in a cage

and starts up again.
'Are you married yourself, *a mhic?*'
'I was never asked.'
'Sure you've maybe no need, you've maybe
a woman who'll do the trick.'

'You know how it is . . .'
I give nothing away, driftwood
on the tide of his surmise
my answers. But I need the ass
and only say 'Be good to that good

woman of yours' though I think to myself
'May your young possess her quality.'
We settle a plan to collect the cart.
He's drunk and I'm linked by one request,
teasing his yes, fending our complicity.

CONFEDERATES

The old ones by the fireside
indent their pensions on hot halves
and launch the week-end in Phil Reilly's.
Workmen come in at lunch-time and suddenly
it's their half-day. Girls come home
from jobs in Dublin, new Persephones.

The boys have watched the river
these past nights and forecast fish;
they've noted times the bailiffs scout
the bridge and banks; they argue hooks
and spears, the proper lamp – the way
they talk you'd need a winch to haul the trout.

In corners lovers whisper oaths,
men hold a glass before their mouths
to tell a comment, episodes,
a neighbour's will, a secret spilled,
'He made it most by spending none,'
Mean? 'He'd mind mice at a four crossroads.'

And was he married? 'Not at all, a family
would need feeding.'
                        There's Bill Tuite,
confined to Coca-Cola, delighting all with wit
and courtesy; the Trapper Cadden, saying
little, watching all – he dreams of terriers,
of digs at foxes' holes midweek, a freer spirit.

We're watching the Sheridan girls, Ronan
and I, and wondering if she'll appear,
the blackhaired girl from Ballyduff.
There's Jennifer, Louise, Iris – their names
like plants' – and boys preparing invitations
bold with wishes, risking their rebuff.

There's Benny Tobin interspersing all he says
with sayings. 'You've often heard it said . . . ,'
'. . . more days nor years,' 'Well now, the way
it is . . . ,' reminding us 'We'll be a long time
dead' and 'wouldn't it be worse
if we could not give out the pay

and *céilí* here and there?' And that man
has the kindest word.
                        The television's
loud though no one looks or listens.
We notice when it's off. We want whatever
isn't there, magnetized by mystery,
and linger after hours, confederate citizens.

Men there all every night greet like long-
separated friends, 'Is it yourself?' 'It was
came in.' 'You're well?' 'There's not a bother
on me.' Talk of weather. 'What time is it?'
'What day is it!' 'It's time to go,
a woman's waiting, time to get the fother.'

Phil's screaming 'Time' and pulling pints.
'Goodnights' all round. Some order cargoes,
six-packs, bottles. There's talk of dances,
discothèques in Kells and Crover, a band
in Virginie . . . an eager hosting slipped
like hounds into the moonlit night, its chances.

Extracts
from a Sporadic Diary

(These entries have to do mostly with the writing of a play which eventually became ARISTOCRATS *and which opened at the Abbey Theatre on March 8, 1979.)*

1976

August 31. Back from holidays and now stancing myself towards winter and work. Throughout the summer there were faint signals of a very long, very slow-moving, very verbose play; a family saga of three generations; articulate people wondering about themselves and ferreting into concepts of Irishness. Religion, politics, money, position, marriages, revolts, affairs, love, loyalty, disaffection.

Would it be a method of writing to induce a flatness, a quiet, an emptiness, and then to work like a farm-labourer out of that dull passivity?

September 1. A. B. describes C. B.'s new play to me as 'a romp'. A curious phrase, attempting to disarm. This is merely to make you laugh, it suggests; the artist is on Sabbatical; the man like yourselves is At Home to you; drop in for the crack.

This is precisely what we can't do. We cannot split ourselves in this way. We must synthesise in ourselves all those uneasy elements – father, lover, bread-winner, public man, private man – so that they constitute the determining artist. But if we attempt to give one element its head, what we do is bleed the artist in us of a necessary constituent, pander to an erratic appetite within us. The play that is visiting me brings with it each time an odour of musk – incipient decay, an era wilted, people confused and nervous. If there are politics they are underground.

September 10. Somehow relevant to the play – Mailer on his daughters: "If he did something wrong, they being women would grow up around the mistake and somehow convert it to knowledge. But his sons! He had the feeling that because they were men their egos were more fragile – a serius error might hurt them forever".

September 17. A dozen false starts. And the trouble with false starts is that once they are attempted, written down, they tend to become actual, blood-related to the whole. So that finally each false start will have to be dealt with, adjusted, absorbed. Like life.

September 30. Coming back to the idea of the saga-drama, maybe even a trilogy with the Clydesdale pace and rhythm of O'Neill. Possibly. Intimidating.

November 3. For some months now there is a single, recurring image: a very plain-looking girl of about 38 – perhaps slightly masculine in her mannerisms – wheels on to the stage her mother in a wheel-chair. Her father follows docilely, like a tinker's pony.

November 7. I think I've got a scent of the new play. Scarcely any idea of character, plot, movement, scene; but a definite whiff of the atmosphere the play will exude. Something stirring in the undergrowth. At the moment I don't want to stalk what may be stirring there. No. I will sit still and wait. It will move again. And then again. And each time its smell will become more distinct. And then finally when that atmosphere is confident and distinctive, I and the play will move towards one another and inhabit that atmosphere.

November 27. "You have chosen to be what you are" – Sartre.

December 7. The crux with the new play arises – as usual with me – with its form. Whether to reveal slowly and pains-takingly and with almost realised tedium the workings of the family; or with some kind of supra-realism, epiphanies, in some way to make real the essences of these men and women by side-stepping or leaping across the boredom of their small talk, their trivial chatterings, etc. etc. But I suppose the answer to this will reveal itself when I know/possess the play. Now I am only laying siege to it.

December 10. THE CANARY IN THE MINE-SHAFT. Title? (It is import-ant when its song hesitates and stops.)

December 15. A persistent sense that the play is about three aging sisters. And a suspicion that its true direction is being thwarted by irrelevant politics, social issues, class. And an intuition that implicit in their language, attitudes, style, will be all the 'politics' I need. Concentrate on the three girls. Maybe another married sister who visits with her husband. Maybe set some years back – just pre-war?

December 17. Endless and disturbed wanderings in various directions, with considerations of masks, verse, expressionism, etc. etc. But the one constant is Judith who is holding on to late young-womanhood, who has brothers and sisters, and who misses/has nursed an old father. THE JUDAS HOLE?

O'Neill: ". . . but O'Casey is an artist and the soap-box is no place for his great talent. The hell of it seems to be, when an artist starts saving the world, he starts losing himself. I know, having been bitten by the salvationist bug myself at times. But only momentarily . . ."

December 28. Judith-Alice-Claire; and Father.

1977

January 7. Making no headway with the new play; apart, perhaps, from the suitability of the word 'consternation' to our lives. I feel – again – that the intrusion of active politics is foreign to the hopes and sensibilities of the people who populate this play.

January 8. The play – this must be remembered, reiterated, constantly pushed into the centre of the stage – is about *family life,* its quality, its cohesion, its stultifying effects, its affording of opportunities for what we designate 'love' and 'affection' and 'loyalty'. Class, politics, social aspiration are the qualifying decor but not the core.

January 10. Going back over four months of notes for the new play and find that the only residue left by dozens of strained excursions is: an aging, single woman; a large house for which she acts as medium; a baby-alarm; the word 'consternation'; and perhaps various house furnishings that are coyly referred to as Yeats, O'Casey, Chesterton, etc. Cryptic symbols that may contain rich and comprehensive revelations – or disparate words that have no common sympathy? So all I can do is handle and feel them. Talk with them.

January 25. Every day I visit the site where the materials of the new play lie covered under cellophane sheets. I have no idea of its shape from those outlines. I can envisage what the final structure may be. But I have no plans, no drawings – only tempting and illusory 'artist's impressions'.

January 31. Is there an anti-art element in theatre in that it doesn't speak to the individual in his absolute privacy and isolation but addresses him as an audience? And if it is possible to receive the dramatist and apprehend him as an individual, is the art being confronted on a level that wasn't intended?

May 2. Mark time. Mark time. Pursue the commonplace. Tag on to the end of the ritualistic procession.

May 24. The play has become elaborate, like a presentation Easter egg. Has it a centre?

May 25. A persistent feeling that I should leave the play aside until it finds its own body and substance. Stop hounding it. Crouch down. Wait. Listen. In its own time it may call out.

May 26. To see the thing exactly as it is and then to create it anew.

June 2. What makes Chekhov accessible to so many different people for 180 years is his suggestion of sadness, of familiar melancholy, despite his false/cunning designation 'Comedies'. Because sadness and melancholy are finally reassuring. Tragedy is not reassuring. Tragedy demands completion. Chekhov was afraid to face completion.

June 21. My attitude to the new play alternates between modest hope and total despair. What I seem to be unable to do is isolate its essence from the faltering existence I keep trying to impose on it. I keep shaping characters, looking for modes of realisation, investing forms – when what I need to do is determine what the core of the play is and where it lies.

September 10. I have a sense that everyone (i.e. all the characters) is ready in the wings, waiting to move on stage; but somehow something isn't quite right on the set. So they drift about, smoking, scarcely talking to one another, encased in privacy. A sense, too, that that slight adjustment, if only I knew what it was, could endow them all with articulacy. Maybe that's the essence of the play: the burden of the incommunicable.

September 17. Six days at THE JUDAS HOLE, when it seemed to take off, not with a dramatic lift, but resolutely, efficiently. And now at a stand-still – that total immobility when it is not a question of a scene stuttering and dying but when the entire play seems specious, forced, concocted. Trying to inflate and make buoyant something that is riddled with holes.

September 18. Moving, inching forward again. But whole areas – central characters, integral situations – about which I know nothing. And my ignorance and their magnitude looming and threatening.

September 26. The play has stopped; has thwarted me. I still work at it. But it sulks. And yet – and yet I sense its power. If only I could seduce it past its/my blockage.

October 17. The imagination is the only conscience.

November 11. On a day (days? weeks! months!) like this when I come upstairs at a fixed time and sit at this desk for a certain number of hours, without a hope of writing a line, without a creative thought in my head, I tell myself that what I am doing is making myself obediently available – patient, deferential, humble. A conceit? Whether or not, it's all I can do.

December 13. "Sometimes, however, to be a 'ruined' man is itself a vocation" – Eliot on Coleridge.

December 16. The dramatist has to recycle his experience through the pressure-chamber of his imagination. He has then to present this new reality to a public – 300 diverse imaginations come together with no more serious intent than the casual wish to be 'entertained'. And he has got to forge those 300 imaginations into one perceiving faculty, dominate and condition them so that they become attuned to the tonality of the transmission and consequently to its meaning. Because if a common key-note isn't struck and agreed on, the receiving institutions remain dissipated and unreceptive. But to talk of 'meaning' is inaccurate. We say "What is the play about?" with more accuracy than "What does the play mean?". Because we don't go to art for meaning. We go to it for perceptions of new adjustments and new arrangements.

1978

February 1. Yesterday I finally brow-beat the material into Act 1. There may be value in it. I don't know. Occasionally I get excited by little portions. Do they add up to anything?

May 19. The play completed and christened ARISTOCRATS.

Three poems

FÉ DHÉIN NA dTIG NUA

Bhíos ann nuair d'éag an t-sráid,
nuair cuireadh fé ghlas iad na botháin:
gruaim 's aoibhneas i gcarcair fágtha,
seomra na breithe, seomra an bháis:
    's go h-uaigneach fé úrláir 's ar falla
    do bhí an luch 's an dúbhán-alla.

Asal 's cárr, barra 's cairt láimhe
ag iompar ár dtocht sinsearach slán leo,
muga m'athar 's mias siúcra mo mháthar:
d'aistríomar gach rud in oíche scathach.
    's go h-uaigneach fé úrláir 's ar falla
    do bhí an luch 's an dúbhán-alla.

OFF TO THE NEW HOUSES

I was there when the street expired, / when the cabins were put under lock and key: / gloom and delight were left imprisoned, / the birth-room, the death-room; / and under the floor and on the wall / the mouse and the spider were lonely. / Donkey and trap, wheel-barrow, hand-cart / safely transporting our ancestral bedding, / my father's mug, my mother's sugar-bowl: / we shifted all under cover of night. / And under the floor and on the wall / the mouse and the spider were lonely.

D'aistríomar gach rud bhí tábhachtach –
ach amháin croí na sean-sráide cráite:
tar éis sos pórtair, chuaig m'athair 's a cháirde
chun é a aistriú cughainn láithreach.
Bhí sé níos mó ná deich gcroí bó,
fearb 's gearb 's créacht air faoi dhó.
Ach d'ainneoin a staire 's a bhróin
bhí forbairt fola beo ann fós.
Go déanach san oíche cuireadh ar chárr é
's tharraing siad é trasna páirce
ach d'éag an croí roimh deireadh slí
's ní féidir linn fós na loirg fola do ní
        's fós go h-uaigneach fé úrláir 's ar falla
        tá an luch 's an dúbhán-alla.

We shifted all that mattered / except the heart of the old tortured street: / after
a pause for porter, my father and his friends went / to move it to us at once. /
It was bigger than ten cows' hearts, / weals and wounds and scabs all over it. /
But its history and grief notwithstanding / there was a living pulse of blood
there still. / Late in the night it was put on a cart / and they pulled it across a field /
but the heart expired before journey's end / and we still can't wash out the
blood-stains. / And still under the floor and on the wall / the mouse and the
spider are lonely.

AN DROICHEAD GO MEIRICÉA

A dhroichid sin 'Briseadh mo Chroí'
minic d'ól tu deora deoraí:
tá do chlocha dlúite le moirteal beo,
uaill na sluaite nach fillfidh go deo.

Na daoine a mhair i mbroinn a bparóiste
(níos sine ná na caisleáin dóite)
bhí ortha éaló thar teorainn
brúite amach le falla deor.

Féachaint thar n-ais níor tháinig ó éinne
ach d'fháisceadar a mbeart le céile
a mbróga leathair thar a scórnaigh,
shiúladar go ciúin tré na bhfearann siógach.

Ba bhás gan aon agó é –
críocha Mheiriceá níos ghoire ná órlach:
's an droichead ag cromadh 's ag cogar
ós cionn abhann mar chearc ar ghliogar.

D'ól tú allas an bhróin go santach
do shúla caoch, do bhéal manntach:
níor chonaic tú do dhaoine ag dul chun ísleacht
i dtreo bun-spéire uafásach na saoirse.

THE BRIDGE TO AMERICA

Bridge that is 'Breaking my heart' / often you drank the exiles' tears: / your stones are compacted with living mortar, / the howling of crowds who will never return. / The people who lived in the womb of their parish / (older than the burnt out castles) / they had to escape over the border / evicted by a wall of tears. / From no one came a backward look / but they bundled their load together, / their leather boots around their necks, / they walked quietly through mysterious domains. / Undoubtedly it was a death – / the states of America but an inch away: / and the bridge bent and whispering / over the river like a hen on a clear egg. / You greedily drank the sweat of sorrow / your eyes blind, your mouth gap-toothed: / you didn't see your people heading towards lowliness / towards the terrible horizon of liberty.

Is annamh a iarrann abha fuil.
Tá, le n-ár dtoil, an breac donn
sa mhargadh ghainmheach: tá ceol
's sróll-ghruaig ghlas: tá áilleacht ann
sa scathán samhraidh, 's um neoin
tugann fáinleoga di a bpóg.
    Pógann gach rud abha.
    Pógann an ghealach í.
    Pógann an sioc
    agus bláthanna crann:
    Pógann an eala í,
    damhsann an bradán innti –
    sinne amháin a mhaslann í:
    le déanaí níor bhfuair sí uainn
    ach bruascar daoine agus mún.
    's d'iarr sí cabhair ón bhfearthain
    's tháinig an bháisteach
    le meitheal uafásach
    's thóg sí a tuarastal,
    cailín amháin.
Thosnaig na cupáin ag clagairt,
rith sruth deora amach na dóirse:
thuit brón ar an mbaile
mar lapa cait ar luch.
Ach tá na h-aibhnte bodhar
agus anois, fásann gruaig órdha
i measc na planndaí faoi uisce.

THE FAIRHAIRED MAIDEN

It's rare that a river asks for blood. / There is, for our pleasure, the brown trout / in the sandy market: there is music / and green satin hair: there is loveliness / there in the summer's mirror, and at noon / swallows give it kisses. / Everything kisses a river. / The moon kisses it. / The frost and the flowers / of trees kiss it. / The swan kisses it, / the salmon dances in it – / only we abuse it: / lately it only got from us / the rubbish of people and piss. / And it asked the rain for help / and the downpour came / with terrible henchmen / and it took its stipend, / a single girl. / The cups started clattering. / A stream of tears ran out of the doors: / grief fell on the town / like a cat's paw on a mouse. / But rivers are deaf / and now, golden hair grows / among the plants underwater.

Three poems

A PEACOCK'S FEATHER
for Daisy Garnett

Six days ago the water fell
To name and bless your fontanel
That seasons towards womanhood,
But now your life is sleep and food
Which, with the touch of love, suffice
You, Daisy, Daisy, English niece.

Gloucestershire: its prospects lie
Wooded and misty to my eye
Whose landscape, like your mother's was,
Is other than this mellowness
Of topiary, lawn and brick,
Possessed, untrespassed, walled, nostalgic.

I come from scraggy farm and moss,
Old patchworks that the pitch and toss
Of history has left dishevelled.
But here, for your sake, I have levelled
My cart-rut voice to garden tones,
Cobbled the bog with Cotswold stones.

Ravelling strands of families mesh
In love-knots of two minds, one flesh.
The future's not our own, we'll weave
An in-law maze, we'll nod and live
In trust but little intimacy—
So this is a billet-doux to say

That in a warm July you lay
Christened and smiling in Bradley.
While I, a guest in your green court,
At a west window sat and wrote
Self-consciously in gathering dark.
I might as well be in Coole Park!

So before I leave your ordered home
Let us pray: may tilth and loam
Darkened with Celts' and Saxons' blood
Breastfeed your love of house and wood.
And I drop this for you, as I pass,
Like the peacock's feather in the grass.

Bradley Court, 1972

SWEENEY ASTRAY

for John Montague

I

As if a trespasser
unbolted a forgotten gate
and ripped the soft growth
tangling its lower bars –

just beyond the hedge
he has opened a dark morse
along the bank,
a crooked wounding

of the silent, cobwebbed
grasses. If I stop
he stops, like the moon
used to.

He lives in his feet
and ears, weather-eyed,
all pad and listening,
a denless mover.

Under the bridge
his pale reflection shifts
sideways to the current,
mothy, alluring.

I am haunted
by his stealthy rustling,
the unexpected spoor,
the pollen settling.

II

I was sure I knew him. The time I'd spent obsessively in that
upstairs room bringing myself close to him: each entranced hiatus as
I chainsmoked and stared out of the dormer into the grassy hillside I
was laying myself open. He was depending on me as I hung out on the
limb of a phrase like a youngster dared out on an alder branch over the
whirlpool. Dream face in the branches. Dream fears I inclined
towards, interrogating:

"Are you the one I ran upstairs to find drowned under running
water in the bath?
The one the mowing machine severed like a hare in the stiff
frieze of harvest?
Whose little bloody clothes we buried in the garden?
The one who lay awake in darkness a wall's breadth from the
troubled hoofs?"

After I had dared these invocations, I went back towards the gate
to follow him. And my stealth was second nature to me, as if I were
coming into my own. I remembered I had been vested for this calling.

III

When I was taken aside that day
I had the sense of election:

they dressed my head in a fishnet
and plaited leafy twigs through meshes

so my vision was a bird's
at the heart of a thicket

and I spoke as I moved
like a voice from a shaking bush.

King of the ditchbacks,
I went with them obediently

to the edge of a pigeon wood's
deciduous canopy, screened wain of evening

we lay like effigies.
No birds came, but I waited silent

among briars and stones, or whispered
or broke the watery gossamers

if I moved a muscle.
"Come back to us," they said, "in harvest,

when we hide in the stooked corn,
when the gun-dogs can hardly retrieve

what's brought down." And I saw myself
rising to move in that dissimulation,

top-knotted, masked in sheaves, noting
the fall of birds: a rich young man

leaving everything he had
for a migrant solitude.

A LIGHTING PLOT
for Brian Friel

Things I saw best when light was rectangular:
A dresser the sun reached framed in door-jambs,
Through a Dutch barn, snowed-in New England farms,
An aerodrome seen through an open hangar.

So not the apron stage: the picture frame.
Under the kilowatts, the croquet lawn,
The lord mayor's parlour, the pub yard at dawn
Act One, the present time. Act Two, the same.

A window pane lies flattening the grass
And the grass bares itself for inspection.
The real is true hallucination.
Spotlight on Christy Mahon's looking glass.

Conquistadores galloping towards straw
Huts of a pueblo have found El Dorado.

Five poems

THE IRISH DIMENSION

With these folk gone, next door was tenanted
by a mild man, an Army Officer,
two girls, a boy, left in his quiet care,
his wife, their mother, being some years dead.
We shortly found that they were Catholics,
the very first I ever came to know;
To other friends they might be Teagues or Micks;
the lad I quickly found no sort of foe.

Just my own age. His Christian Brothers School
to me seemed cruel. As an altar boy
he served with dread. His magazines were full
of faces, places, named, unknown to me.
Benburb, Wolfe Tone, Cuchullain, Fontenoy.
I still am grateful, Willie Morrissey.

THE PRISONERS ON THE ROOF

A hundred yards along the other side
from where our house stood ran the high gaol wall,
dark, grey and blank, with everything to hide
save at the clanging front-gate where they call
with captured men in vans. So, once, just then,
the cells were crammed with gunmen – I.R.A. –;
their protest they asserted in a way
proclaimed though they were captive, they were men.

For they had thrust and clambered to the roof,
and clattered, rattled chamber pot or pail –
all metal instruments they find in gaol –
to keep the town awake when all should sleep.
We heard the rumoured uproar, ran for proof;
and thought the ledge they danced on high and steep.

A CASE OF MISTAKEN IDENTITY

We heard a rumour, ran to swell the crowd
down at the far end of our avenue;
for in an empty house, a woman vowed,
a vicious gunman hid; it could be true.
Someone already had reported it;
the soldiers had arrived. A young man tried
the door, was warned, persisting, stept inside.
The stout police sergeant urged us back a bit.

There was a burst of gunfire, sudden, clear;
we could not see but judged it very near.
The young man had run through the back door
and opened it. And from the entry's end,
behind the houses, soldiers fired before
he'd chance to show he was not foe but friend.

from a sequence 'The Troubles 1922'

THE MAGICIAN

So Uncle Sam was truly Prospero,
that house his island palace. There I shared
his marvels and his magic. Thence I'd go
with netted rods and jam-jars well prepared,
to pace the tow-path by the drifting stream,
or step through heather for the furtive moth.
I gaped to watch his magic-lantern beam
figure with life the hoisted table-cloth.

His nimble fingers thrilled the mandolin,
or strummed banjo. Once, with a pointed blade
he gouged a fist-sized eagle from tough oak.
He glittered through my days, a paladin
in all accomplished, nature's tricks his trade,
till one sad day, for me that dream-spell broke.

CONSEQUENCES

Our houses parted as that shutter fell
in this same town. Not once I'd race again,
close on his heels, along a tufted lane,
net at the ready. Nevermore he'd spell
Darwinian theory from a mollusc shell,
nor cruel logic in the spider's skein.
Yet from that teeming mind there must remain
much which has made and kept me infidel.

He'd taught in Sunday School, had been expelled
for heresy, since Darwin's was his book;
from thence his reading went from bad to worse.
So, though I lost him early, I have held
close to that sceptic and enquiring look
at the old riddle of the universe.

from a sequence 'My Uncle'

from

Retrograde Canon at Atepmoc

from DOG-DAYS, a *novel*

THE DOGS OF ATEPMOC

The dogs of Atepmoc, the most silent breed in the world, give tongue loud and aggrieved when kicked, as if no dog had ever been kicked in Atepmoc before. But is it not rather their proud and contentious spirits that have been abused and not their canine nature, considering that they hardly behave as dogs at all? The ones that guard the flocks do not behave *as one would expect,* protecting the wings and rounding up strays, but slink along with vacillating tread more like soldiers behind gun-carriages at state funerals than dogs herding goats. On the skyline, almost home, posed in heraldic style, dexter paw raised, they scarcely resemble dogs; and in this I believe they imitate the leading goat, a bearded ram with a tangled span of horns, the pro-genitive parts protected in a leather truss; becoming more and more hesitant as they near home, pushing forward only to stop, hesitating, as if uncertain of their whereabouts, or their welcome.

Stray sheep with long unclipped tails move among the main goat-herds, the frisky half-grown lambs steal the ewes' milk on the sly; among them also pigs, self-sufficient and busy as only dirty pigs can be.

Dried skins of snakes are prized as treatment for mules with the colic. To *think* of a fox (na orroz) is considered to be an unlucky omen. The herdsmen, powerful sling-shots, carry furled black umbrellas when foul weather threatens and, sometimes, transistor sets.

THE VOICES

The voices of the males are rough. As boys they had perhaps shouted to each other overmuch in the hills, argued the toss too heatedly in the blaring bars, smoked too much strong black tobacco (Ayog), drank too deeply of the potent local wine, orange-hued and midway to being sherry, that produces ulcers.

The young males cluster together and jeer but keep to themselves, congregating above the Azalp meeting-place and the promenade called Oesap, sheltered by plane trees, from where on a clear day it is possible to see the Dark Continent in the form of the Salta Mountains, the oldest in the world.

The womens' voices are most raucous in the morning, pulling one (by the roots) out of the deepest slumbers, as the pitch of their excitement rises, their fury one might think, if you did not know them; so that surely blows must follow. But no, the early arguments end in high-pitched screeches and good-natured morning banter. They are both simple and baffling.

Stout Allemrac, mother of two hairy sons, loudest and merriest of all, and old childless Adnanref with the blind spectacles and a twisted knee, her husband dead of cancer, leads the screeching.

Women beyond child-bearing have registers of the highest pitch, as if in a state of perpetual wonder and bewilderment, *permanently* surprised. The younger women, particularly the girls waiting for marriageable males, are quiet and rather withdrawn, speaking hardly at all; the formally engaged ones retreat even further into themselves, possibly obsessed with trousseaus. Some head of cattle, a rough breed, are now kept and can be heard bellowing in the ravine near the kahl-burner's cave.

Send us canorous! Here even the mountain streams are noisier than elsewhere.

FIRE SUPERSTITION

Fire (Oguef) has a different meaning, another secret power. I saw a little girl dancing in a fire. At the all-night kahl-burning, women with their menses must keep away. The log on the open hearth is embraced by arms of fire, split in twain by fire. The tree struck by lightning ignites in the storm at night, in torrential rain, burns away an area to the dimensions of a football pitch, watched from the high road as it happened, seen some days later, a burnt-out area among evergreens. The word for fire is the same as the words for "game" and "play".

THE TOWN'S REFUSE

They have no nightcarts or refuse collection as such, but with little or no regard for hygiene, all the refuse and filth of the place is flung into two narrow gorges situated at either end of the uptilted village. Acac is *shit* with all that it implies, though "Aveun acac!" (with a brandishing of the right fist and a rolling upward of the eyes) is regarded as a friendly greeting. (The refuse piles in the ravines, with dead or dying animals, might be regarded as their version of our professional thieves, soiling unspeakably the collected linen of a robbed house, "posting a sentry").

They have Evil Eyes painted on the bottoms of their chamber-pots.

SOME OBSERVATIONS

They are very superstitious, believe in ghosts ("the Other One"); carry heavy old-fashioned black umbrellas as people unaccustomed to rain, although it rains torrentially through January and even February. The postman, a hopeless drunkard in green gumboots, is seen disappearing into the mulemen's bar and that's the end of the postal delivery for the day. His customary greeting to me: "Yoh adan!" (Today nothing!). The drunken barber brandishing a cut-throat razor, leaves a customer profusely bleeding, only shrugs his shoulders. Adan! again: hypnotic stasis.

It is close to impossible to embarrass or get a rise out of them, though it can be done. When overcome by embarrassment (but on your account), and really put out, they show it by absenting themselves, slowly averting the head and lowering the eyes, with all the monumental dignity of dumb brutes. It may rankle for a while and will then be overlooked and forgotten in as far as such breaches of manners can be forgotten. In the quiet end-of-season time, given over to flies and hunters out after "nogidrep" (a sort of partridge), the same hunters seldom sober by evening, the old men play a game like dominoes in the small main Azalp, and card-games everywhere, or rather one single game, a game without numerals.

DEATH OF AN OLD MAN

Some days ago an old man of eighty years died when crushed by a backing truck and pinned against the wall of the raisin factory. All his life had been spent in that vicinity near the dump and there too he had died, pressed in against the sunny wall where he had liked to take the air. Some years before, after betting on a single lottery number all his life, he was called away to sick relatives and gave up his number to an unmarried officer of the Civil Guards, whereupon his number came up and the delighted bachelor received one million Sgita. The old man gave up buying lottery tickets. In the manner of his going, the village expressed neither sorrow for the one nor censure for the other (a youth who had no licence), believing that chance prevailed to a great extent and one could be sure of nothing, except that one would die one day. Adan (nothing), it was a word often on the lips of the women; no doubt the main tenet in a daunting philosophy that kept them all in such fine high spirits.

ITS AMBIENCE

How soon the voices cease and evening silence falls! Among the group on the wall below, waiting for their evening meal, the stories become bolder as darkness came on, and it falls suddenly here. Two glasses full, two empty, two glasses refilled here on the terrace; below they drink nothing. Now comes the turn of the planet Venus. "Eiram, Eiram, euq ecid?" (Marie, Marie, what are you saying?) "Arim em, Eiram!" (Look at me, Marie!). Soon they retire and the wall is empty. Darkness falls on Atepmoc. Even the cuckoo in the olive tree behind the house falls silent. Do cuckoos call at night? Always silent at night. A curious lone bird, when one calls, is it to another, or for themselves alone that they call out with the strangest of all bird-calls, in these hills at least, odder than the Ocip sohics (fig pickers) who whirr in the air in October. *Messiaen* heard an unknown bird calling in Persia, in the evening, and put it into his hymn-work as the voice of God, not thunder but a voice close to silence, and therefore nearer to God, one can safely assume. The silence that now on the terrace falls, and on Atepmoc below, is an intimation of the great silence that will one day descend and never lift again. The globe and its wretched burden of history was only a dream, a bad dream only in God's head, on an off-day long past, now whirled into space, nothingness.

ATEPMOC IN OCTOBER

It is fine weather now, the sun very hot during the days and cool in the evening. You can see the currents in the sea some thirty kilometers below us, down the valley beyond the hill-villages (Solbeups) called El Clot (where they cast stones at strangers), Ab Oxú (ill-lit and dry all summer) and Nulles (haunt of half-wits who throw stones at each other), and the sun goes down very fiery. Getting dark earlier, the two buses coming home with their lights on, ascending all the time, around more than two-hundred curves.

The colours of our Autumn sky change all the time, minute by minute. The sun goes down and a breeze starts up, the light goes out of the sky, the mountains darken, the enoirrogs (a type of sparrow) end their chittering and depart, leaving droppings like small burnt worms on the terrace. Then the evening ritual of the goats going by, heraldic beasts leading, the main herd anxiously emitting dry farts, knowing home is near. That's how it is in Atepmoc.

The Abbey in Those Days

a memoir

JUST OVER FIFTY YEARS AGO I happened to be directing a rehearsal of our National Theatre Company in its first presentation of *King Lear* when I was interrupted by a message from the Box Office to the effect that a Mr. Shakespeare wished to speak to me on the telephone.

As might be expected I was somewhat taken aback by a call at this time from such a source. So, suspending all operations on the stage, I hurried to the receiver in the front hall only to find that it was not, as feared, a stricture from another world on my treatment of the play, but an enquiry from a local photographer of the same name as to when it would be convenient for him to come and take some pictures of the production for publicity purposes.

Needless to say I was somewhat relieved at this discovery, and I listened attentively while he described how on a previous occasion both he and his equipment had been accommodated on a number of planks placed across the seatbacks in the Parterre, from which elevation he and his valuable camera had been precipitated into the narrow space between the rows owing to the unexpected disintegration of the platform. He hoped that a disaster of this kind was not going to occur again. Nowadays in the reconstructed Abbey, there are no such hazards in the taking of production pictures under proper auspices, but in the heyday of Mr. Shakespeare there were peculiarities in the old building that affected not only photography but also the presentation of many of the plays themselves.

It is well known from many published works that the handsome, sober-looking grey building in Marlborough Street that came to be known as the Abbey Theatre had previously been a morgue, notwithstanding the fact that it bore on its parapet a carved inscription reading SAVINGS BANK – surely a rather cynical expression, however it got there, to apply to a repository for broken bodies! What is not so widely known is that the operative part of the interior, as we came to know it, had nothing to do with a morgue, but for many years had been a centre for popular Vaudeville, opening off Lower Abbey Street, and known as The Mechanics' Institute. It already had a small stage, and no doubt other facilities for the refreshment and entertainment of the Mechanics of its day.

How this strange combination of buildings came to be amalgamated into the original Abbey Theatre by its most assiduous, non-paying member of the audience, the late Joseph Holloway, is a matter on which very little information is now available. All that is clear is that the morgue provided the principal entrance hall, the box office, a tea and coffee bar, a repository for hats and coats, a short flight of stairs up to the theatre's gallery, and a few steps down to the stalls. Upstairs in this front building the offices were to be found, together with two or three extra dressing rooms and possibly some lavatory accommodation, although personally I cannot remember ever having found any such convenience.

The Mechanics' Institute provided the auditorium and its two principal peculiarities: firstly that it lay at a right angle to what was now its main entrance, unusual in a theatre, and secondly that the stage backed on to a public lane, which still runs down the blind side of the present building. This meant that no extension could ever be made to the depth of the playing area, which when combined with the absence of any facilities (apart from a narrow lighting bridge) for flying scenery, had a noticeable effect on the structure for most of the plays written for the theatre by the more experienced Abbey playwrights. An interesting academic thesis will no doubt be written some day attributing Yeats's adoption of the technique of the Noh Play to the difficulties raised by the birds required to be flying overhead in his *The Shadowy Waters,* while there was always a difficulty in the last act of *The Plough and the Stars* in shooting Bessie Burgess through a rear window thanks to that immovable back wall.

Nevertheless in spite of this bagful of technical problems, the Abbey achieved its world-wide fame; and this in a Playhouse where it was advisable for all major exits to be made on Stage Right for the simple reason that on that side there was a wide and capacious scene dock, into which even a motor bike could, if necessary, be ridden into the distance – (as occurs in George Shiel's *The New Gossoon*) – while on Stage Left there was little room left for any sort of exit apart from a short flight of steps up to a tiny· hall; the rest of this particular area was usually regarded as the sacrosanct property of Barney the Prompter and U. Wright, the electrician, one of the most traditional members of the company who was usually asked to play small but important parts which required his constant appearance on the stage as well as his attention to the switch-board. (His 'U' actually represented "Udolphus", his Christian name, although Yeats used to refer to him regularly as "Uranus".) It had also to be remembered when planning movements on the stage that, for some unknown reason, the arch of the proscenium had been planned (or left from other days) between eight or ten feet off centre of the stalls, which left a considerable portion of the stage out of sight of customers seated at the left end of the front rows.

Apart from these problems there was, however, a pleasant sociable sort of life back stage, with friends of the players visiting the Green Room even during performances. This was a feature that was not usually frowned on by the authorities – as would certainly be the case today, as the stage was well within earshot – and the Old Troupers of the company were well able to keep a familiar play going with a few gag lines while some missing party dashed down a short flight of stairs muttering "Excuse me. That was my cue". More serious was the problem presented by an occasional visitor who, on entering by the doorway from the lane, would find himself unable to get to the Green Room without crossing the stage, and might indeed do so while the curtain was up. Even this intrusion has been known to be covered up by somebody speaking an additional line such as: "Oh yes. That was the brother I mentioned. He's just coming back from Mass." They were real Pros – that small pre-war company!

And let it be remembered that in spite of all these perils and handicaps, the management of this "National Theatre Society", whose premises went up in smoke about twenty years ago, survived at least three departures of most of its principal players to pastures elsewhere. It faced two riots and recognised two Nobel Prize-winning authors. It also defeated two determined attempts at mob censorship, not to mention a third by the Lord Lieutenant . And all of this to the music of a very accomplished five piece orchestra, intruding on the front row of the stalls, while delighting the public with everything from Bach to Antheil.

One other feature does remain, however, apart from this courageous tradition – the familiar insignia that is to be seen on all its old programme covers and that still ornaments the notepaper and flyleafs of its more prosperous successors. There are some who insist that the picture is supposed to represent Maud Gonne – a lady who protested more often than she played: others insist that it is Cathleen Ní Houlihan. For years until recently, nobody has been able to say who designed it, and now I am afraid that it has slipped my memory again. Anyhow, this figure is of a good-looking girl, stripped to the waist, and holding in one hand a somewhat out-of-date bow and arrow, while she fixes her black hair with the other. Meanwhile, she is either urging on or restraining an Irish wolfhound from attacking the sunrise. Or maybe it is the sunset. A somewhat ambiguous picture that may be intended to influence the pit or reassure the stalls – whichever way you may interpret it.

Let us end by comparing this image with the escutcheon of the very competent offspring of the Abbey's Peacock – the Dublin Gate Theatre – a playhouse that used to be noted, amongst other things, for the length of its performances. This other design has been interpreted in the malicious way of our native city, as representing Micheál MacLiammóir, dressed as Harlequin·and trying to prevent the curtains from closing in time for all of us to catch the last bus home.

Extract from a Novel

"THERE IS NO NEED TO LOOK SO MISERABLE," said mother.

Constance didn't answer. She stared across the drawing room at an unfamiliar figure in the gilt framed glass above the fireplace. Hair prinked, seed pearls strangling the thin neck, yellow dress and lipstick, just a touch of lipstick. Woeful eyes stared back at her.

"You look as if you're going to be executed, for heaven's sake."

"I don't think yellow suits me."

"Nothing'll suit you if you continue to look so disagreeable. Smile or something."

Both yellow figures smiled at each other.

"That's better."

A lie, thought Constance sourly. Somehow things hadn't seemed so bad up in the dimness of her bedroom.

Mother sighed.

The door opened and Bibi came in. Her dress wasn't yellow. It looked marvellous.

"Have a glass of sherry, dear, and tell Constance not to be silly. She says she doesn't want to go."

"I've never wanted to go. You blooming well insisted. I can't stand Patricia O'Mahony. I hate all that *slow, slow, quick, quick, slow* stuff and this is a horrible dress."

"Nonsense dear, it's sweet. Isn't it sweet Bibi?"

"It's a pity it's yellow," said Bibi unhelpfully.

"Don't be unkind, Bibi." Mother had a glimmer of a smile on her face as she spoke.

"You'll have a lovely time. Don't brood dear, never brood at parties. Just keep smiling."

"It looked all right in the shop."

"If you like," suggested Bibi, very kindly, "I'll let you borrow my blue taffeta."

"No. Don't encourage her Bibi. She looks perfectly alright as she is. She just has to pull herself together."

Constance turned away from the glass. Blue taffeta, yellow moiré, it didn't make much difference.

"I bet Ingrid Bergman never looked like this," she said.

Bibi laughed. Mother tutted and went and poured herself another gin and tonic.

"The great thing is . . ." There was a hissing sound as she unscrewed the top of the tonic bottle ". . . to feel you look marvellous and then everybody else thinks you do. I look marvellous. I am marvellous. It sort of flows out of you towards them and they, they become . . . well, engulfed in it. It's all a sort of confidence trick really. I am marvellous." She put the bottle back on the tray and took a sip of her drink.

"I am marvellous," sang Bibi and did a *slow, slow, quick, quick, slow,* across the room. She was wearing a pair of mother's pre-war black satin evening sandals with little diamanté buckles on them that sparkled as her feet moved.

Father put his head round the door.

"Ready girls?"

He came into the room.

"How stunning. How scrumptious you both look. Dear me, Constance, how grown up you are. You'll take the sight out of their eyes." Constance blushed and felt the trembling and the blur of tears.

"It makes me feel so old. Two grown-up daughters. Dear me."

He didn't look old, greying a little behind the ears, but only in the most distinguished way.

"Not a chick left in the next. I won't be back before eleven, dear. I told Henry Barrington I'd pop into the club and have a word with him about this damned case of Herlihy's. Alright girls, coats on."

As the two girls went out into the hall Constance heard her mother's voice, low and cold.

"Just as long as you're home before the girls."

"Ridiculous woman."

I'm going to take *boom* boom a sentimental journey *boom*

Gonna put my heart at ease
Gonna take *boomboom* . . .
Straight from the bath, ears, nails, eyeballs shinily scrubbed.
A sentimental journey . . .
Faces scraped, soap smelling,
To renew *boom* . . .
Young men from the safety of their numbers, glasses clamped
between damp fingers, eyed the butterfly girls.
Oh, memories. *Boomydaboom.*
Massed flowers in the corners of the room trembling to the
music. Girls massed by the azaleas trembling also in fear that they
might . . .
Oh, God, please God . . . be left, yellow or blue or green,
alone by the flowers.
Red wine, white wine, on silver trays, and tumblers of cup
filled with cherries, oranges, apples, mint leaves, lemon slices,
meals in themselves.
Boom boom a sentimental *boomy.*
Will you er . . .?
Gonna put my *boomy boom* . . .
One and two and sorry.
Do you hunt?
No.
Boomy crash
I say, sorry.
To renew old memories *bang bang* crash.
Thanks awfully.
Back to the azaleas.
Old, old, young men hardened by the Battlefields of Europe
squashed their cigarettes out in the flower tubs and laced the cup
with whiskey from the hip flasks hidden in their inside pockets.
Oh sleepy lagoon *tar a* the moon . . .
Frightful band.
And two on an island . . .

Bibi's diamanté buckles glittered everywhere.
Dee da dee dee da
Oh sleepy lagoon . . .
You Barbara Keating's sister?
Yes.
Oh.
And two on an island . . .

You in Trinity?

No.

Oh.

Jolly good band.

Oh sleepy lagoon . . .

Oh, God, let it end. Let Bibi suddenly want to go home. Headache, tummy ache, broken leg. No such luck.

Thank you so much.

Bow ties wilted, like the flowers, or crept sideways leaving adams apples climbing out of tight white collars.

Old, young men cantered on the floor, hot cheeks pressed against the hot cheeks of girls who had never thought to death or battlefields.

Young, young men, licked their lips nervously and concentrated on avoiding their partners' feet.

Scrumptious food, don't you think?

Are you going to the Bradleys on Thursday?

No.

Oh.

There's nothing left for me of all that used to be . . .

Do you hunt?

No.

There's just a memory among . . .

Slide two three, *glide* two three,

My souvenirs.

Sorry.

My problem, thought Constance with certain anguish, is that I would like to be enjoying myself, but I can't. Why? Why can't I? Ooops.

Sorry.

Take your partners for the *Walls of* . . .

Hurray. Push up there a bit. Here. Hands, hands. Great fun, this.

Limerick.

Daaaaa.

Dawn spreading into the sky. Brave stars still sparkle like diamanté shoe buckles.

Good night ladies, it's time to say goodnight.

"Don't tell Mummy I danced all night with Charles Barry."

Sleepy sparkling eyes.

"Who's Charles Barry?"

"Sssh."

"Why not anyway?"

"Sssh."

"Bibi?"

"Ssh, I said, sssh. You'll wake them. He's divine."

Black satin slippers dangling from her hand. Diamanté, stars, eyes . . .

"But . . .?"

"Ssh. He digs with the wrong foot."

Good night ladies, it's time to say goodnight.

She

an unfinished story

THE DIRECTOR IS WALKING AROUND in circles talking about the last scene. He takes the last scene first for a reason I don't understand. He's trying to explain to them the key to the whole thing, which is at the point where the girl walks to the cross-roads to meet the young priest, all ready to tell him she won't go with him after all, but the priest doesn't turn up so the girl says her message to a man she doesn't know, a man that's just passing by. She repeats it over and over but the man just stares at her. Then the man walks off and the girl is left just standing there saying nothing and at this point, the director says the light should fade just a little and the film is to be about that light fading more than about anything else. My father nods his head and agrees and says the film is about the light fading and the knife the priest used in the third scene, not about the girl or the schoolteacher or the priest. He says the director should film it backwards is just as break-up-able as space, that that's such a cliché now it shouldn't need to be repeated. His hair has gone grey now, not all grey, just grey at the sides. I think he likes it grey, I think if it wasn't grey he would dye it grey anyway. I think he has wanted to have grey hair ever since I knew him and now that he has it he is more pleased than he has ever been, which is not much. He wanted to be grey like that, to talk like that, to be thin and distinguished like that so when he talked everybody would listen. He wanted to be like that since he was born because he knew then people would look at him, and listen to him without turning round and talking to someone else.

I walk away from the set and lie down beside the caravan that is used as a canteen. The grass is flattened here by the tyres of the camera trucks, it is flattened like a bed, I stretch out my legs on this straw bed and roll my levis up over my knees. My knees are like big dimples, my legs are slim and brown with the sun of the last few days with spines of tiny hairs all along the shinbones. I think of those hairs, I think of my father's hairs, I think how pleasant the sun is.

They tell me I have a peculiar quality of lightness, he says he wants to capture it, the lightness in the way I walk, the way I say lines without moving my face or my body. I think of this and I feel light, as if the grass is not really bent underneath me but each blade is just tensed lightly, holding me who am so light. And we have waited three days now for the sun to fade to just that quality of light that he says the scene demands, since he can't afford false light and the film is about the light fading more than anything else. So we rehearse it during the day for the evening take, we go through it falsely, waiting for the perfect falsity of when the light fades. I am a girl who sits in the glass cabin of a petrol-filling station somewhere in the country on an empty road between two towns. I was picked up by a traveller who later deserted me and in the scene, the last-but-one, I sit in the cabin again waiting for a man to pass, my hand round the butt of a heavy German Mauser pistol, in an open drawer and when the arbitrary man passes I raise it and shoot through the glass panel of the cabin and the glass windscreen at his astonished face, shattering all three. Then I drop the gun and stare with a deadened blankness at the road I have always stared at, the cars coming down it from one town, going to the other, their dimmed lights coming on now. And I stare at the lights as if they were messages I am beyond reading.

I get up from the grass, I take out a *gauloise* from my pocket, the packet is crushed, the sun is covered by one of those white cumulus clouds so the heat is gone. I light the cigarette as I walk back over to them, the man who could be my father with the grey sidelocks, the youngish Londoner who's directing, short and perceptive with cropped hair, boyish clothes. He has that London quality I've always admired, a kind of tired, wry decadence, affluent and beyond affluence. He sees the world through opaque lenses, is universally and meaninglessly polite, gives an impression of being constantly engrossed in some personal tragedy that probably doesn't exist. I suspect he's homosexual but so far he's shown no antipathy to me. And so I tell myself I like him, I tell myself I like them both, my sympathy amazes me.

Three poems

ALWAYS

It will always go back
To a big man hunched in pain over a phone,
Smoking, waiting for news from Cork,
A brown envelope containing
Stamps of Sarawak,
Talk, on the landing near the room
Where I awoke, sweating,
Of freak weather hitting the South,
A forefinger touching a scar
Like a sign of friendship
Made after war,
The first taste of blood in the mouth.

It will always go forward
To a man standing over a grave
Acknowledging a woman,
A woman standing over a grave
Acknowledging a man,
Both rotten, having remembered
The privilege of being forgotten
By children, friends, the faithful stone,
The patient acre fertilizing every sin,
The river joining the sea's voice
Like the pair of them standing at the door of the house,
"You're welcome, welcome! Come in! Come in!"

THE PILGRIM

I see a girl climbing the mountain
In a red blouse and blue jeans
Rolled up to the middle of her shinbones,
No shoes on her feet meeting the sharp stones,
Climbing among rocks, a smile on her face
Though her mind may be bleeding from old
And new wounds. In time, she accosts the saint
And in the silence a story is told,
A drop is added to the deepening sea
At the top of the mountain before she
Faces down to the world from that brief height.
Below her, for miles around, the fields
Are graves for sheep that never saw the Spring light
In grass kneeling to receive the bones and skulls.

GODDESS

Look at her—nothing that isn't gold
Or hint of gold in some unquestionable way,
Content to shed her light into the world
Making the comely light of day
Sluttish by comparison.
She smiles in mercy at the thought
Of any rival. Suppose a doubting man
In some understandable manly fit
Took a knife and plunged it through her
The blade perhaps a measure of his lust
To touch the secret of her tireless light,
Would he kneel forever in despair or prayer
To see her light turn to a winter night,
Her beauty a stone that, touched, is dust?

Homeward Bound

Part of the opening of a novel to be called, perhaps,

NOTHING HAPPENS IN CARMINCROSS

TEN MINUTES OUT FROM KENNEDY AIRPORT he discovers that the man sitting beside him has no legs. The take-off is effortlessly accomplished on the seven Brandy Alexanders he has taken in the El Quixote on Twenty-third Street, and the three taken in the airport to reinforce the seven and for luck, one for the Father, one for the Son, one for the Holy Ghost, and to keep the kindly courageous glow from dying inside him. Not till the fire is dying on the hearth seek we our consolation in the stars. If he had been a glutton and/or if he'd had a little more leisure he could have filled his belly and, with twenty Brandy Alexanders, or Brandies Alexander, he could have flown the Atlantic without benefit of aeroplane. He is a big bald man but that is still a lot of brandy. Who the hell anyway was Alexander? Which Alexander? The man from Macedon? A good title for a new musical with Julie Andrews double-rôling as the lovely Thais and St. Cecilia, sharp violins proclaim. Or the man from Ulster who did all the generalship for which Montgomery (another man from Ulster whose mother he had once seen stopping people on a Donegal road and handing them bibles) took the credit? Or was it the Alexander who owned the ragtime band? Or Alexander Korda? Or Alexander Knox who, in a movie, pretended to be President Wilson? Or Alexander Pope?

He sits right in the front of the plane, in the Vippery, in the best seat.

In the tin sheds that were cinemas in his boyhood the best seats were at the back. You went there to Saturday matinées in the fond, seldom or never realised, hope of groping Loreto girls sprung for the afternoon from the penitentiary of the convent boarding-school, the holy house of Loreto carried by angels over land and sea. He unfastens his safety-belt when the girl tells him he is free to do so. A command or permission so worded would, long ago in the dark cinema, have provoked outrageous hilarity: unfasten your safety belts, young ladies of Loreto.

The girl in the plane also gives him a large brandy, no Alexander, paid for by the airline because he is up front and a Vip, God help us, and little does the girl know and he already awash like the ocean below him: brandy to brandy, dust to dust, and bugger the broad Atlantic.

In all honesty his safety-belt hasn't been all that exactly fastened. His stomach is too ample and neither is the man beside him a slim boy, even though the seats in the Vippery are wide like the Brenny plains in old Pádraic Colum's song, the contiguity is embarrassing. Now as he struggles to push the unfastened belt out of the way he upsets the rug on his neighbour's knees (he is about to think) and see that he has no legs and consequently no knees. As well as which, his neighbour clutches in his left hand one of those white enamelled vessels, shaped like a carafe gone askew, oddly called bottles, into which bed-ridden patients piss. Out of fellow-feeling he looks the other way.

A second girl, hostess, stewardess, Irish and lovely, readjusts the rug, removes the bottle delicately covered with a green cloth, a priestess bearing away a veiled sacrament. The first girl brings him another brandy. The second girl comes back with a fresh bottle or the same bottle emptied, rinsed, sterilised, as good as new. When this act of removal and renewal happens for the third time in thirty or less minutes he follows the girl up to the door of the sanctuary where the bottles are emptied. He says: Look, excuse me, but I spent a year or so in hospital once myself and perhaps I could look after my neighbour's little needs. It might save you a spot of trouble.

They love him – there are three of them - big and bald as he is. Perhaps they love him all the more because of his baldness, fatherliness, grandfatherliness. Also: they hadn't bargained on so many bottles. He goes back to his seat. He empties and rinses bottles at intervals of from ten to twenty minutes, slowing up somewhat as they sweep eastward, on and on, high up with the sun, towards Europe. . . . Every time, almost, he empties a bottle one of the grateful girls brings him another brandy. He eats well when the food comes. As a volunteer bottle-emptier he has a larger ration of Beaujolais than any Vip among the Vippers. He could achieve drunkenness but he has a big stomach and a large bald head, and he is there when he is needed and carries the bottle as if it holds elixir or ichor itself, and he remembers the lovely young nurses who had carried bottles, and worse, from his hospital bed. In those enthusiastic days, when the touch of a hand on a knee could result in a horn, it was scarcely possible to insert oneself into the enamelled orifice of the bottle, feeling it carefully first for chips, abrasions, cutting edges, without allowing the mind to toy tenderly with the thought of the fair hands that rinsed and sterilised it, pale hands I loved, and all that, beside the Shalimar. The thoughts of youth are long long thoughts, said Longfellow, and a good man too.

Peoria, Illinois, his neighbour says.

Then a long time afterwards: It was a rail accident, both legs destroyed, the bladder too.

Then much later: Compensation big but what the hell good is compensation?

Finally: Relatives in the County Carlow. Haven't seen them in generations. They'll be at the airport. It'll be good to see Ireland again. The last Sunday before I left home there was snow on the ground, a light skiff of snow. The brother and myself coming from Mass, tracks of a hare in the snow. We followed it over seven fields. Often wondered when I was in the hospital after the accident did the hare ever realize that he had written his death warrant with his own legs.

The only story he can think of to cap that one is vulgar, trivial and most inappropriate in view of the relationship the fates have set up between himself and his neighbour. . . .

No, under the circumstances, and since he had not gauged the delicacy of his neighbour's humour, that story will not do: all the brandy in France won't make it apt. So they don't talk much. So many stories and *bon mots* seem, *ipso facto*, barred. You can't even say the hostesses have lovely legs. He pours out piss and rinses the bottle and drinks free brandy. He pisses now and again himself so as to be in the swim and watches with mellow eyes the secondhand brandy go the way of all water. He tells his neighbour that he is going north when he gets to Shannon, to the wedding of a niece in a place called Carmincross: also to see his aged mother and, between one thing and another, and going to Guatemala once, and Mexico and Alaska at other times, and even though it is a swift business to cross the Atlantic nowadays, he hasn't been home for four or five years.

Once he dozes for a full five minutes, but comes coldly awake and with a most guilty feeling for that he is the slave of the lamp, the djin out of the bottle and has no liberty to sleep. Thereafter his catnaps are briefer, a minute or two at a time, never taking him quite away from the naked sun outside the plane, from the jet-drone that could be a sound of his own body. He nods and starts up again, nods and starts up again, in and out of the same continuous vinous dream: he is a young sailor on the deck of a windjammer sailing east for Ireland, the white sails fill, the deck sways like all adventure, the long green-and-purple headlands of Cork and Kerry reach out over the water to touch and welcome him: green green was the shore though the year was near done, high and haughty the capes the white surf dashed upon, dashed upon, upon. He is awake again and emptying another bottle. . . .

– Not long now, he says to the legless neighbour. Two hours to Shannon.

Delicately he nibbles or nipples at a new brandy and is back again on the windjammer but not, this time, as the young sailor. He is too old, feeble – and thin, for Christ's sake, his arm is around the young sailor's shoulders, his boy's voice that had long ago learned the poem from a schoolbook which he can see open and dog-eared on the little table beside the brandy, his boy's voice coming out of the aged body and asking the sailor to hold him up so that he may after all these years see Ireland; as a starveling might stare at the sight of a feast. Forty years work a change. When I first crossed the sea, there were few on the deck who could grapple with me. But my youth and my pride in Ohio went by and I've come back to see the old land e'er I die. He sank by the hour, and his pulse 'gan to fail as we swept by the headland of storied Kinsale. . . .

Kinsale, Kinsale, and he is wide awake, grasping his brandy with expert cunning, muttering to himself, sensing the sweet South that breathes upon a bank of violets, stealing and giving odour. It is the perfume of the first girl. She is bending over him. She is smiling. She says: do you come from Kinsale?

– No. Much further north is my place. But I do like Kinsale, the history, the headlands, the long twisting inlets, the sunset on the Bandon river.

– It's a swinging place now, sir, you wouldn't know it, tourists, yachts, new shops all arty-craft.

He agrees that he mightn't. She has a Cork accent. She wears an engagement ring. She will be married next spring. He tells her that he is going to the wedding of a niece, his favourite niece, one of five sisters: once I was in London with her, he says, we met an old friend of mine who said with a leer that he supposed this would be my favourite niece. And she said: it so happens that I am his favourite niece.

They laugh at that and the man with no legs laughs with them. It isn't really noticeable yet, but he knows they are going down, pay the first nodding respects to the earth that has nourished them: crowded, talkative Cork, fertile Carlow and the great Barrow river, far Fermanagh, a filigree pattern of lake and water meadow hooked on at the west to the lonely Cuilcha mountains. He empties another bottle. He says to himself: This must be my last brandy.

For he has promised to wheel the neighbour out to meet the waiting relatives and to be drunk in charge of a wheelchair would not look well. He has no catnaps now, no dreams good or bad, just gentle free-wheeling memories, a boy on a bicycle again, as the plane slackens speed, tightens reins so that you can feel it, as if it wanted to turn and go back to the smells and confusion of New York. Down there below the clouds Shannonside air will still be clean and breatheable, he'll be able to pump the gasolene and whatnot from his lungs.

Down we go to Ireland, spokes spinning and humming, never when I was young did I dream I'd free-wheel down a hill thirty thousand feet high: six Scotch firs, humpbacked, bald patches on their heads, gesticulating in the wind in a gossiping huddle at the top of the hill, a winding river in the valley below, and a white creamery with red-rimmed windows and a high shiny cylindrical chimney ejecting puffs of steam, two thatched cottages: writing a fragment of a sort of doggerel verse in my head as three of us, school-friends reunited, scorch down that hill: All day long our whirring wheels sing their song, and there steals on the air every scent of the spring. Oh the tingle of wind in the hair as we speed without heed down the hills, and the rush and the race and the pulse and the pace, and three friends, parted long, met again in the spring, and do you remember an inn, Miranda, and so on and so forth. . . .

The second girl goes up the plane saying: Fasten your safety belts.

from

Her Whiteness Attracts a Blackness

an extract from a novel

LET US SAY (AS THEY SAY) that she was born in 1936. I was born in 1934. She Libra. I, Virgo. Little differences like these may yet allow me freedom of her. She was in Switzerland in 1956. While I was in Dublin. She travelled timidly (I begin to see her, now, for the first time) shoulders hunched as if to draw-in her breasts, towards which she had ambivalent feelings, her old blue suit-case, the one (which one?) with the rims helplessly rising to either side, like ears, her brown tweed coat home-made from a suit-length bought at the Woollen Mills, her new cotton dress, white with purple flowers, her awkwardly daubed lip-stick which didn't quite match anything. A migrant teacher of English abroad, quaking before all prospects on that efficient grey train speeding through Valais. Oh, such specifics!

In other words she is a version of myself although I never made such a journey in 1956. Unless it were my daily stagger to Parson's Bookshop in Baggot Street in my one, ugly, cheap suit, my insecurities leaking at the cuffs, to steal a read from books. *Universitas mundi!* Why I've had to concoct her at all must wait for the moment. It is certainly not enough to say that by making me into a her when in fact I am a he, allows me to conceal the personal. Something of that, yes, as always but more, much more. For instance there is the familiar twitch of fiction, her coming into being only when I lie effectively. She is a kind of falsification of everything that is or was. Yet she alone can corroborate everything I have ever known about anything written of in these pages.

Well, then. She returned to Dublin sometime in the sixties,

around about the time that I set out myself into Europe, different if complementary routes, Spain, Greece perhaps, perhaps Jugoslavia. Does it matter? Places I could write about, if necessary. And with an almost no-change to show for the interim. I mean in me, therefore in her.

I have decided to make her a teacher like myself, creatures of ink and chalk and time-tables, reciters of the lives of others to others, talking down from a height in quotations, talking back from a distance to those behind. That was it, the teaching! It was like a raft for me (therefore for her) for years: classes from nine to four, lunch-break, tea-break, polite demeanour, regularities, regulations. It held together above some kind of flood, year after creaking year, for me, for her. I mean I will make it so. Down below a blood-sea surged, turning and rolling in the darkness. When my (her) raft finally broke-up that viscous tide devoured the timbers and I was able to record her (my) fiction. And this is what this is all about.

Who needs a simile? Tell it as it is or was or will be in the pages following. So: the story, as they say. Angela Kirwan, twenty years old, leaves Ireland to teach in Switzerland where in a period of a few months she comes to know something of love, exile and aloneness, at some point in the company of an exceptional if dishonest man, quite some years older than herself. I provisionally call him Mr. Butler out of a kind of kinship to a character in an earlier novel of mine. And is that all? Not quite. She returns home having suffered a glaze to cover what had been, after all, a traumatic experience so that for eleven or twelve years afterwards she fitted into a daily routine (the teaching, the flat on Leeson Street with her friend Mary, the pictures, the dances, the dates, the odd dinner in the Shelbourne Grill) a teacher in a Dublin convent school. Then, again as they say, (I will work out the details of this later) something split open inside her and she became Another, a shadow figure rising up inside her (which she in some way welcomed as a kind of sister) possessing her, driving her to act after act of courage against everything she had been up to this, and even as she felt her old self disintegrate under the onslaught, she became increasingly aware (surrounded at that stage by nurses, nuns and Doctor Mac in that Dublin clinic) that what was happening to her was a disordered reliving, recovery even, of that long-ago year in Switzerland.

That she has never existed outside these pages, then, is immaterial but that she has begun to exist on them my heart pounds out this nervous proof: ignorant of the shape of her jaw, the expressions of her mouth (for the present, for the present) I can still plunge my hands into the blue suit-case at her feet (say on the quays of the North Wall, Dublin, a wet night, 1956, the start of her journey) and rifle the laundered contents: the handkerchiefs, the underwear stitched and restitched, the long woollen shifts, remnants of adolescence, which her mother (Who is her mother?) in flushed exchanges insisted upon her including ("It'll be cold in Switzerland, Angela. Sure look at all that snow over there!"). And then, yes then, tucked away in the bottom of the suit-case, an old biscuit tin, decorated with the faded outline of roses and pastoral ladies suggestive of a dance but not dancing because they were seated and inside the box, a tangle of threads, needles, clasps, pins, one unmended rosary beads, faint odour of face powder while under all of this like a lover's secret the simple mortuary card with the face of her dead father, scissored from his wedding picture, grey thin moustache, pale eyes, choking white collar, a white flower in his button-hole. Inscription: "Patrick Joseph Kirwan, Kildoddery, Clonmel, County Tipperary, who departed this life, July 6th, 1944. RIP."

She never knew this face (remembering her father as different) except as framed by the buttons and ribbons of her box. Until she was fifteen the card, as one would expect, had lain with the other novena and prayer leaflets between the pages of her missal, unexamined by her in her daily use of it, its prayer with crimson initial capital letter already stored, like her other daily prayers, in her memory, repeatable like a rhyme: "We give them back to Thee, O Lord, Who gavest them to us. Not as the world givest, givest Thou, O Lover of souls. What Thou givest, Thou takest not away. And Life is Eternal and Death is only an horizon and the horizon is nothing save the limit of our sight. Lift us up, strong Son of God, so that we may see further, yea, even beyond the horizon to where our loved ones are with Thee. Amen".

When about her fifteenth or perhaps her sixteenth year she removed the card from her prayer book to bury it in its hiding place in the old Jacob's biscuit tin, she was at first unaware of a motive. But having done it, her daily communion with the grey face, even without the card, continued, the words of the prayer rolling their vowels in and out of her every-day and she became frightened by the molten, indistinct images that began to present themselves to her. Taking her problem first to the confessional she found she was unable to explain herself. The priest, a kindly man, insisted that it was a good thing to pray for the dead, especially one's own dead. She turned instead to her mother who, quite unaccountably, began, fluttering, head turned aside, an incomplete explanation, at least six weeks too late, of menstruation, to the dazed and white-faced girl, repeating again and again the apparently relevant comment that "If your father was alive he'd like you to grow up a good girl, so he would". And years later Angela was to marvel at this odd treatment for her distress, since her nightmares and daypanics did indeed stop after that and the face of her dead parent moved further off beyond the grave.

And so on and so on and so on. I could go on like this (like what?) indefinitely, incident by more or less credible incident, faint echoes of where things have come from, pages perforated from other files, objects found and stored (Here is the mortuary card that I have used for the above, that of a relation of mine that I scarcely knew) on and on and on, why, why because I cannot have relief nor she the once angelic Angela release until I can store away in her shape, as securely as forgetfulness, to become as harmless as dust, a legion of old spirits etcetera. 1956. 1956. What I believed then, 1956, to have been a violation of myself, what I later learned was an invitation to becoming which I fled in terror at the time, fleeing from a fear of myself into the ordinary, the routines of what is called normality until the dyke inside me burst and in the bloody flow I tumbled back to that year but not just I, this time it was she, I had found her in me, that was me, then, could see her (me) undergoing the old story again, but the old story utterly changed, it being tellable because it was now different, made into a meaning, at last, in the finding in some recess of my skin of this pale-green Angela-shadow (From what rib has she come?) like a leaf orbicular, petaloid, with that perishable incidence of mortality at the root of her stem. Also courage, for all that frailty, some fibre through her system that allowed her to endure what I could never endure (at least without her in me) so that now, my life collapsing I have the strength to write her into existence, a modest effort compared to her courage in carrying my lost self into such depths.

The more I compound her differences to me the more she assumes everything that I cannot express of myself. I never encountered the equivalent of her sauve, if balding seducer, Mr. B. of Switzerland (that mild tragedy, that pale circumference of suffering which surrounded them both). Nor have I ever seen that school of hers in the Alps, those clumsy brothers in charge, the old mother, those pampered children from three continents who disturbed her classroom. I never had a friend like her friend Mary in Dublin. I did not end-up as she did, or will in the pages following, in that Dublin clinic for mentally disturbed women, the rattle of minds, the cubicles of perspiration and groans, the gloom of Doctor Mac with his note-pad and struggles to remain in advance of his procession of nurses and nuns, the one man in that house of women. Nor have I known two such as Tom and Dick, contrasting lovers who accompanied her part of the way down in her last reckless assault upon what she had been. All, all fabrications in my own milder progress to the point at which I can begin to write about them. In the immortal words of the epigraphist: *All names, characters, and events in this book are fictional, and any resemblance to real persons, living or dead, which may seem to exist, is purely coincidental.*

Four love poems

literal translations from the Irish

I

My own dark head (my own, my own)
your soft pale arm place here about me.
Honeymouth that smells of thyme
he would have no heart who denied you love.

There are girls in the town who are vexed and angry
– they tear and loosen their hair on the wind
for the dashingest man in this place, myself!
But I'd leave them all for my secret heart.

Lay your head, my own (my own, my own)
your head, my own, lay it here upon me.
Honeymouth that smells of thyme
he would have no heart who denied you love.

II

I would I were in England
and one from Ireland with me
or out in the middle ocean
where a thousand ships are lost

with the tempest and the rain
to drive from wave to wave
– O drive me, King of Heaven,
to where my love lies down!

Remember that night
      and you at the window
with no hat or glove
      or coat to cover you?
I gave you my hand
      and you took and clasped it
and I stayed with you
      till the skylark spoke.

Remember that night
      when you and I
were under the rowan
      and the night was freezing?
Your head on my breasts
      and your bright pipe playing . . .
I little thought then
      that our love could sever.

My heart's beloved
      come some night soon
when my people sleep,
      and we'll talk together.
I'll put my arms round you
      and tell you my story
– O your mild sweet talk
      took my sight of Heaven!

The fire is unraked
      and the light unquenched.
The key's under the door
      – close it softly.
My mother's asleep
      and I am awake
my fortune in hand
      and ready to go.

IV

If you come at all
come only at night
and walk quietly
— don't frighten me.
You'll find the key
under the doorstep
and me by myself
— don't frighten me.

There's no pot in the way
no stool or can
or rope of straw
— nothing at all.
The dog is quiet
and won't say a word
— it's no shame to him:
I've trained him well.

My mammy's asleep
and my daddy is coaxing her
kissing her mouth
and kissing her mouth.
Isn't she lucky!
Have pity on me
lying here by myself
in the feather bed.

from

A Walk on the Cliff

a story

ORDINARILY MAUD DROVE LIKE A FURY. Today, longing to see her daughter again, she threw her luggage into the boot of her car and was on the road well before the hour suggested by her son-in-law. She was longing to see Veronica again and wanted to arrive early to see their house by daylight, and the view. Speeding through the midlands, she was indifferent to the beauty of the fields lit by the rich, yellow sunlight of the early Autumn day. She was very happy. She had not seen her daughter since the day she watched the happy pair drive off after their wedding, a troupe of slightly tipsy young people running down the driveway after the car, and bombarding it with confetti. In the intervening months her heart had ached with a loneliness no letters, no phone calls, could assuage.

Even as a child, Veronica had tried to take her dead father's place, and striven hard to cope with what Maud acknowledged to be her many failings. Nicest of all, the girl made light of those failings, ash in the coffee cups, pencil parings in the hand basin, that sort of thing. How Maud missed her; she was not fool enough to think that her loneliness would be cured by a quick overnight visit, but it was her own wish to stay only one night. Veronica, and Denis too, had pressed her to stay longer, for the weekend at least, but she'd been adamant, although her visit was long overdue.

The newly-weds had got it hard to find a house in the city of Waterford. They had to stay in a hotel for six weeks. When they finally hit on a house, it was eight miles from the city, in a small fishing port, which was also a popular family resort. Maud could guess what that meant – plenty of beds at a low rent. The same families had probably been going there summer after summer for years. And if a family did defect, the owner of the villa would have a long waiting list of other families suitable in need and kind. Veronica had written that the owners were chary of anyone looking for rental on a year-round basis. Accommodation was harder to get in winter than in summer, because owners, mostly pensioners of one kind or another, depended for a semblance of home life on claiming back their properties in the off-season. No doubt they spent the dreary wintry months attempting to stave off the total collapse of their dilapidated villas, foraging in junk shops for spare parts of electrical appliances no longer on the market, or conning inventories in hopes of getting compensation for sofas and soft coverings damaged not by tenants but by Time.

Veronica and Denis were lucky enough to find a villa whose elderly owner had to go to Jamaica for an indefinite period to care for a brother unexpectedly invalided. According to Veronica the sole merit of the villa was its availability, but that could hardly be true, Maud thought, since it was at the sea. Surely that counted for something?

All her life Maud had yearned to live by the sea, but she had invested so much of herself in her home and her beautiful garden, she could never seriously contemplate moving. How she loved the sea, though! When the signpost showed she was nearing the coast, she slowed down to catch the first glimpse of the ocean. To her surprise it had been in sight for some time. She had taken sea for sky. What she mistook for flecks of mist were waves capped by an off-shore wind. There was a mist gathering. She stopped the car at once and got out to fill her lungs with salty air, half-hoping her ear might catch the boom of surf. Not near enough for that, she continued on her way.

The day was changing rapidly. Arriving at last at the port, which was smaller than she expected, she found it lay between two headlands, and a real fog had collected in the hollow. She changed into first gear and drove slowly down the main street, on which the entire community of villas seemed to be congregated, all much of a muchness, weatherbeaten and depressing. Any number of these shabby villas could have been called yellow. Any number had ramshackle verandas. And all the gardens were the same, a straggle of fuchsia bushes, a dismal array of puce petunias while in front of every hall door there was an apron of ill-assorted pebbles and crushed sea-shells, obviously barrowed up by hand from such stretch of fore-shore as one must surmise to exist here somewhere. Not finding the house, she was forced to turn the car on a cement ramp that evidently ran down to a harbour, because she could see the top of a lighthouse, over a shambles of shacks, sheds and warehouses, which hid the sea itself.

Voyaging back along the street a second time, and forgetting she had arrived earlier than expected, Maud felt Veronica could have been more helpful with her instructions, when, suddenly she heard Veronica's voice and joy with a rush flooded over her.

"Mother! We didn't expect you for hours! How did you make it so fast? You must have driven like a demon." Appearing out of the least likely of the villas, Veronica was struggling to wrench open the corroded iron gates, but before Maud could get out to give a hand, she gave up on it, and ran out. "Let's leave the car on the street. Denis can bring it in later," she said airily and leaning forward she gave Maud a kiss.

Maud was somewhat taken aback. They never used to bother kissing. "Stop fussing, dear" she said. She was attempting to get out.

Veronica stood back obediently enough, but she glanced at her little wrist-watch.

"When did you leave home?", she asked, but she didn't wait for an answer. "You really drive too fast Mother, I worry about you". She took Maud's arm, but when slightly upset by a new, matronly tone in her daughter's voice, Maud disengaged her arm to lock her car, she frowned. "There's no need to lock it, Mother. We never lock ours. This is the safest place on earth. Come inside and have a drink – unless you'd prefer tea?"

"Oh, tea is a nuisance," Maud said. A cup of tea would have been nice, but Veronica would undoubtedly feel obliged to provide all the paraphernalia of saucers, spoons, a cream jug, a sugar basin. Anyway, just then Denis appeared, and from Veronica's shriek of surprise, Maud guessed her son-in-law had come home early in compliment to her. His greeting was as cordial as anyone could wish, and she liked the masterful way he put out his hand for the keys of her car, yanked open the gate, and drove the car in to the hall door. But when he opened the luggage compartment and she saw his look of stupification at all the puck she'd brought, she was embarrassed. Veronica only giggled.

"Don't be alarmed, Denis. Mother always takes as much stuff with her for a night as for a week."

Maud had a moment of compunction. She saw no point in packing properly when travelling by car. She just flung a few jumpers and undergarments into one case, and things likely to crush into another. Jars and bottles, which might spill, should always be put in a case to themselves.

"There's no need to bring in them all," she hastened to say. "Just that one." She pointed at random to one of the cases, trying hard to remember what it contained. "And perhaps that small one," she added apologetically, thinking she might have put her sleeping pills in it.

"You must need them all when you brought them all," Denis said proceeding to unload everything methodically.

"Well not that one!" Maud said, pointing out a fourth case. "That one is empty." She turned to her daughter. "You know how it is, Veronica? An empty case can come in handy if . . ."

But Veronica was peering into the boot.

"What on earth have you got in those cardboard boxes, Mother?"

"Which ones? Oh those! Those are some of your wedding presents that you left behind. I thought . . ."

"That was very thoughtful of you," Denis said politely, but he looked very relieved.

Veronica was now poking about among the boxes.

"That can't be ours, the seal isn't even broken," she said, impenitent. She had the grace to blush however, when she saw the carton bore the label of a well-known wine merchant. Maud turned to Denis who had left the cases in the veranda and was now about to lead her into the house. She pulled back.

"Aren't you going to lock the car?" she said,

"But it's inside the gate!" he said.

"Your wedding presents are still in it!" she said. "Not to mention the wine!" To avoid further argument, she whisked the car keys out of his hand. "If you don't mind!" she said . . . .

Four poems

THE WHITE BUTTERFLY

I wish that before you died
I had told you the legend,
A story from the Blaskets
About how the cabbage-white
May become the soul of one
Who lies sleeping in the fields.

Out of his mouth it wanders
And in through the eye-socket
Of an old horse's skull
To explore the corridors
And empty chamber, then
Flies back inside his lips.

This is a dream and flowers
Are bordering the journey
And the road leads on towards
That incandescent palace
Where from one room to the next
There is no one to be seen.

When I asked you as a child
How high should fences be
To keep in the butterflies,
Blood was already passing
Down median and margin
To the apex of a wing.

The sexton is opening up the grave,
 Lining with mossy cushions and couch grass
This shaft of light, entrance to the earth
Where I kneel to marry you again,
My elbows in darkness as I explore
From my draughty attic your last bedroom.
Then I vanish into the roof space.

Wrapped in brown paper like a present
Your ashes lie above his skeleton.
Yet only last week you were my mother
And he, until nineteen years ago,
The early riser on Christmas mornings
And inveterate poker of fires,
Ears tuned to the shifting cinders.

I have handed over to him your pain
And your preference for Cyprus sherry,
Your spry quotations from the *Daily Mail*
With its crossword solved in ink, your limp
And pills, your scatter of cigarette butts
And last-minute humorous spring-cleaning
Of a corner of a shelf in his cupboard.

You spent his medals like a currency,
Always refusing the third light, afraid
Of the snipers who would extinguish it.
Waiting to scramble out of the shell hole
Hand in hand with him, you imagined
A Woodbine passing to and fro, a face
That stabilises like a smoke ring.

OGHAM STONE
i.m. Seán O Baoill

This is the only headstone I can make.
Your epitaph gets lost between the lines
I compose in a forgotten alphabet,
Ogham notches, a score you hardly hear,

A keyboard upended in the grazing
Now that the repertoire goes underground,
A scratching post for cattle, an outlier
That gathers in a circle other stones.

COMMUNICATIONS

I

My own voice is the echo on the line,
Elderly after a round-the-world trip
To the kiosk where we talk for ever,
My head connected to her sleepy head.

II

Cut off by a blizzard of pieces of paper,
Love letters written during a postal strike,
I have resorted to rumour, bush telegraph,
The risk of messengers becoming the message.

III

Because we are living in a hollow
There is a double image on the screen
And we receive the ghosts of ourselves
From the ground above us that interferes.

IV

I have been tapping the distances between us,
An engineer at his ease up a telegraph pole
Or a saboteur galvanised on the power lines,
Wedding ring and buttons soldered to his skin.

Bachelard's Images

I   The Cottage in Winter

He dreamed of a house in the woods,
a cottage shooting rings of smoke
through winter snow, like sea gulls
banking through the loneliness
of the ocean. He *imaged* that house
as a ship, or a smooth lover,
a place that remembers its inhabiting.

And afterwards he discussed Memory—
how, in the deepest dream-centre
of the world, the home, all lost loves
and the bright blue light of initial
child-habits would find togetherness:
each in the house of his childhood
would relive the fruitful idleness called love.

II Nests, Shells

Look at the bird trusting a tree!
That nest in the fork is all female,
if we stretch out our hands we touch
its cosmic sincerity. Would a bird
build without agreement, without instinct?
No need to test a tree, to question love
about the origin of its confidence in the world.

Even shells pulse and rejuvenate; winter
and summer they follow the cosmic rhythms.
A roof that grows with its inhabitant,
it is the coffin's enemy; its hidden life
is always planning resurrection. Listen!
Listen, it places us forever between
what is manifest and what is hidden.

Three poems

CEOL NA dTÉAD

Sular rugadh Críost nó Crom
cuireadh an geata úd faoi ghlas;
sular stealladh an fhuil cois Simöis céin
cuireadh Fearfeasa san bpoll faoin scraith
is rug sé rún na h-eocrach leis
chun Hades thíos isteach.

Ach ar neamhchead cháich is saoithe Bhín
d'oscail an port faoi lagbhrú do láimhe
gur nochtaigh garraí i radharc do shúl
nach raibh nimhlus ann nó nathair,
aon samhlaoid drúise nó ciarscáth sceimhle
nó taidhleoir an bháis ag siúil
ar bhánta, ach

Órféas, éigeas, sheas ann 'na aonar
is cruit óir Thracia i ngreim a ladhrach,
is gach fidil geilt dár chaoin ariamh
thar iatha allta na hUngáire
i bport a bhéil ghil . . .

STRING MUSIC

"Before the birth of Christ or Crom, / yon gate was locked", they said; / "Before
blood soaked the sands of Troy / the secret of its golden key / passed with its
keeper beneath the sod; / it lies in Hades to this very day – / Word in the mouth
of its voiceless dead." / But in spite of mob and Viennese sage / that gate swung
open beneath your touch; / a garden opened to your gaze / that harboured no
serpent, no gapwinged bat, / no shadowed image of terror or lust, / no willow
stalking among its trees; / Orpheus, poet, stood there alone, / Thracian lyre in
his hand's firm grip . . . / And in his bright mouth's song you heard / every
insane violin that had ever sobbed / across the wild, wild plains of Hungary . . .

FÉILEACHÁN

Ardód chuici, adúras,
íobairt dharaí gach féith . . .
Béarfad chuici
(baoth mo mhian)
tintreach reann
na n-oileán mara,
driogaí maotha
na gcaonach aille is
ogham fada foighneach
na feamainne . . .
Ac níor shéideas ariamh
stoc na gréine
go buacach
thar a sneachtaí léimeach';
níor cheansaigh gaois
nó giodam a goirme
faoi shrathar smísteach
smachtach
ár scéalna . . .

Gach tráth d'fhéachas
lem' íota a shásamh
le fíon gléineach a lámha
thugas cealgaireacht aolta
na dúirlinge faoi deara –
siosúram neamhstaonach
idir í is m'éisteacht,
is m'fhéachaint a mealladh
ag sobal a éithigh,

a féileachán
ag princeam go giodamach uaim
i dtiachóg mhear na gaoithe.

BUTTERFLY

I will raise to her, I said, / the oaken sacrifice of every vein . . . / I will bring to
her / (a foolish whim) / starry lightning / of the islands of the sea, / tender pangs
of the cliff mosses, / the long patient hieroglyphic / of seaweed; / but never have
I blown / the trumpet of the sun / in triumph over / her tumbling snows / nor
tamed either depth / or soaring height of her blue / with the hard-edged /
wounding reins / of our myth . . . / Each time I sought / to satisfy my thirst / with
the bright wine of her hands / I have been faced with / foreshore conspiracies
without cease, / the unending sigh of sand / between her and hearing, / my eye
entranced / by the foam of her illusions, / her butterfly / dancing away from me
skittishly / in a swift wallet of wind.

EADARTHEANGACHADH

As cláirseach gan sreang
atá ceol an fhómhair
ag siosarnach anuas

siollaí faoi bhalbh-íonadh
ag cruinneáil ag na crosairí

is tádar ar a dtáirm anocht
"donn" agus "buí" á rá acu
de chogar
na cainteoirí dúchais seo
gan fiacla

ach ní thuigir a dhath
ná bac
is gearr eile a mhairfidh siad

agus tá feadóg gan pholl agam
ar a gcasfaidh mé
(duitse ach go h-áirithe)

an port
        ceanann
céanna.

TRANSLATION

From a stringless harp / autumn music / buzzes down / syllables in dumb surprise / gather at the crossroads / they're doing their best tonight / these native-speakers / sans teeth / "yellow" and "brown" / they whisper / and you understand nothing / no matter / their days are numbered / these days / I carry a chanter without stops / on which I shall play / (for you especially) / that / selfsame / tune.

Four poems

UNTITLED

I would commission for you
An alphabet of portraits from A to Z;
Then, with a curator's surveillance,

Award them proper names and fixed addresses.
When you delayed last night
Outside the college gates, drenched to the skin,

The shop front windows shone, a gallery
Emblazoned with Rubens'. Gazing at you,
I would give it an Impressionist title—

Girl Sitting Under A Tree,
Small rain blown out of the branches
In a watered blue, like an eye filling

Beyond commentary. What I want
Is a catalogue to that anthology
Of moments like the minutes between showers

Where I can stand, no connoisseur
But a Middle European who restores old pictures
Hesitantly, and without irony.

This one that I'm working on, I'd name it
Girl In A Shop Buying Clothes,
From the studio of an apprentice,

As you prance about in front of a mirror,
Helpless, choosing a blue dress,
And driving me to tears.

TALISMANS

A heretic looming out of flame,
My father plunges through dwarf forsythia
To plant a birch on my fifth birthday. I
Hunker at a seed-box as his spade sorts
Dirt from a crushed Norse collarbone.
"Touch it! Touch it!" till I must imagine
Blades lungeing like sky on a side-glance,
Or break loose, being too imagined by them:
But store it, talisman, in a coat pocket.

My uncle strokes it at a funeral,
Salutes to a volley of shots, quoting
"I Am Of Ireland". He recalls
Cells shared with the Chief, bedding
That concealed keys. Kneeling, I listen
As shovels collect old cloth, prise loose
Space for the coffin. Once home,
An Irish in his fist, he gropes in drawers
Blindly, for the sealing wax that sprang him.

Lastly, I must match his brother's bullet:
A chaplain prowling shell-holes to pick
Discs from the tucked faces of small soldiers,
He sprawls here, playing deaf, on a buttoned couch.
Behind which, in a white Communion suit,
I crouch to build a house of cards—
Precarious storeys, Joker, Ace—
For billeting my tokens: bullet, bone;
Wax in the mould of their impressions.

AFFIDAVIT

E vidence mounts: that notelet on your desk,
Theatre tickets in a coat pocket;

Your photo as a book-mark in my study;
Three blond hairs in a hair-brush. Whose?

Habitual clues no-one makes anything of.
The book is near completion, first

Hearings point to a body in a bed,
Yours, the love-victim, in sleep stirring.

Throat marks, a creased pillow prove it:
My hand is everywhere in this.

Courts of enquiry that I set up grant
Pardon upon appeal. Still, daily,

I am committed to trial, to fresh
Verdicts and new sentences.

I solve the riddle by accepting it
In this sworn statement of our mystery.

NEIGHBOURS

Years they have stood around me, totems,
Mouths drawn rigid in a red zero: their
Throats chuckle and drool. Timid at ovens,
Buttocks absurdly tilted, a moor salaaming,
Or pitched from windows, the blinds handclapping,
What deafened to obscurity, outstared them?
Clamour of children, the earth calling; shriek
Of vertical trees dying from the sky down?

Years I have pestered them for a sign,
Hungered after a hand-clasp or a mouth-kiss,
The cheekbones moist as stone. They shy away,
Are stone-shapes twitching with the pain of tissue.
They hold fast to their last words, they leave me
Agitation of water, windows blown wide,
My lips bent upon words, deep wound of the mouth.
Now I would not presume upon them, grudge

That solo flight, a wrenching into wholeness,
But bind, swab, staunch, most closely minister.
I might long since have howled my way to silence
But found the cry cut short by paper turning
Lithely its wrists in a language of the dumb,
Luck in the knowledge of the password. Had
They spelled it out! The broken skin of pages
Healing all lesions, slow ointment of names.

JOHN MONTAGUE

Poems from Section III ('The Black Pig') of

The Dead Kingdom

THE BLACK PIG

. . . one sees that the Battle is mythological, and the the Pig it is named from must be a type of cold and winter doing battle with the summer, or of death battling with life.

W. B. YEATS

I have arranged to increase the animosity between Orangemen and the United Irish. Upon that animosity depends the safety of the centre counties of the North . . . .

GENERAL KNOX, MARCH 1797

Ballinagh, its flat, main street;
that sudden, sharp turn North.
Nearby, a ridge of the Dunchaladh,
the Black Pig's Dyke, or Race,
—the ancient frontier of Uladh.

Straying through a Breton forest
once, I heard a fierce scrabbling,
saw his blunt snout when
with lowered tusks, a wild boar
ignored me, bustling past.

And can still believe in
some mythic bristled beast
flared nostrils, red in anger,
who first threw up, where North
crosses South, our bloody border.

(Or some burrowing Worm
slithering through the earth
from Ballinagh to Garrison,
a serpent's hiss between
old Uladh and Ireland.)

And now he races forever,
a lonely fearsome creature,
furrowing a trough we may
never fill; the ancient guardian
of these earthworks of anger.

BORDER

That wavering needle
pointing always North.
Approaching our Border
why does my gorge rise?
I crossed it how often
as a boy, on the way
to my summer holidays,
and beyond Aughnacloy
felt a sense of freedom
following the rough roads
through Cavan, Monaghan,
greeted at a lakeside orchard
where we stopped to buy
apples, Bramley seedlings,
Beauty of Bath, with
its minute bloodstains.

But by the sand-bagged
barracks of Rosslea, Derrylin
the route is different.
Wearing years later
I go North again and again
—Express bus from Dublin,
long car ride from Munster—
to visit my mother while
she wastes away slowly in
a hospital in Enniskillen:
learn the bitter lesson
of that lost finger of land
from Swanlinbar to Blacklion.

Under Cuilcagh Mountain
inching the car across
a half-bombed bridge,
trespassing, zigzagging
over potholed roads, post-
boxes, now green, now red
alternatively halted by British
patrols, unarmed Garda,
signs in Irish and English,
both bullet pierced, into
that shadowy territory
where motives fail, where
love fights against death,
good falters before evil.

THE PLAIN OF BLOOD

Near here, he stood,
    the Stooped one,
Lord of Darkness,
drinker of blood,
eater of the young,.
King of the void,
The Golden Stone.

But are such visions
of an abstract evil
an evasive fiction:
the malignant Cromm
but the warming sun,
his attendant stones
the whirling seasons?

The evil sprang from
our own harsh hearts:
thronged inhabitants
of this turning world,
cramped into a corner,
labelled by legend,
Ulster or Northern Ireland.

Source of such malevolence,
a long nurtured bitterness.
No Nordic family feud,

arm & thighbone scattered
(the ravens have gorged
on a surfeit of human flesh)
but wise imperial policy

hurling the small peoples
against each other, Orange
Order against Defender,
neighbour against neighbour,
blind rituals of violence,
our homely Ulster swollen
to a Plain of Blood.

THE WEB OF MAN

A rainfall of blood
from the clouded web
on the broad loom
of man slaughter!
Slate armour gray
the web of our fate
is long being woven:
the furies cross it
with threads of crimson.

The warp, the weft
are of human entrails.
Their severed heads
dangle as weights,
blood dark swords
are spiralling rods.
The arrows clatter
as the furies weave
the web of battle.

The land of Ireland
will suffer a grief
that will never heal.
Men, as yet unknown,
who now dwell upon
wind lashed headlands
will hold the nation.
The web is now woven:
The battlefield crimson.

from the old Norse, 11th century

But who does not fear
     the bristling boar of death
the bustling black
     hog of his own death,
stained tusks, with
     all that huge weight
of deadly muscle?
     Hooves pounding in
the reiterated nightmare
     of my friend O Riada:
breathing and bustling
     out of our dark past
to harry and haunt him:
     the shapely young hero
dying, from thirst,
     his white thigh gashed
under the still brooding
     helm of Ben Bulben,
Fionn, his old friend
     and enemy, near him.

Fionn's hand was stayed
     by a poet, from slaying
the snoring MacMorna;
     Fame lasts longer than
any single life,
     never use treachery:
the poet's morality
     overthrown by jealousy
in this dark valley.
     Three times he allows
the water of life
     to spill from his palms.

Do pale horsemen still
     ride the wintry dawn?
Above Yeats's tomb
     large letters stain
Ben Bulben's side:
     Britons, go home!

from

Prologue '68

a novel

WEDNESDAY WAS A SLACK NIGHT in 'The Devon Rooms', which meant that it was just possible to move from the front entrance through the long bar and the Singing Room and out into the back entry without being smothered in the crush of bodies or, if one was not a *habitué*, asphyxiated by the strange fumes peculiar to the place. On Wednesday night, too, one stood a better chance of actually reaching the front door without injury, the gauntlet of blue-faced youths who clustered on the pavement and prowled the vicinity being proportionately less than on other nights of the week. The wear and tear on shoe leather, however, was about the same, the entire area coated in a corrosive, stitch-rotting paste consisting of urine, spew and copious spillage of the speciality of the house. 'The Devon Rooms' was the only pub in Ireland devoted exclusively to the dispensing of cheap, rough cider – 'Scrumpy'.

   The three elderly men who now entered and moved in single file through 'The Devon Rooms', as they did every Wednesday night, wore thick gumboots. They all remembered when the house had been called simply 'Slattery's', after its owner, now dead. Then it had been ill-lit, dirty and all but deserted six nights of the week, a homely place frequented by confraternity men from the nearby chapel, lapsed Pioneers on the run from other parishes, and quiet conspirators. When old Slattery died, young Slattery had come home from England with the idea of making a quick killing by means of buying in bulk and selling cheap the West Country product for which he had developed a mild liking. Years later, alas, he was still here, that mild liking now an insatiable craving, his middle-aged face the deepest blue of all, nodding respectfully from behind the bar as the three sober old men passed through to the Singing Room.

The sights and sounds of the long bar were one thing – the din of insane hilarity from the dark snugs; the thud of fists and crashing of glass as big men pounded one another senseless, all the while laughing –, they had become used to these: the Singing Room was something else; one never knew what to expect . . . To-night they were dancing; half-a-dozen couples shuffled around, supporting one another, the ladies as blue-faced and dishevelled as the men. In a corner of the room a man sat playing a piano with such great gusto that it must have been ragtime. But no one beyond himself – or the dancers, perhaps, by way of some alcoholic telepathy – would ever know . . . for there was no music . . . because there was no piano.

"Sacred Heart of Jesus!" exclaimed the first man to emerge into the back entry, pausing to wipe the steam from his glasses with the fringe of his muffler. He was short and stout, tightly packed into an ancient Dexter, his bald head clothed in a black beret.

"It's worse than the Brasso," said the second, clearing his nose, finger and thumb style, with a flourish. He was a skeleton under the false bulk of his Hong Kong parka, his plaid muffler crossed defensively at the throat in a way that cast doubt on there being a shirt underneath. He had had resort to the Brasso himself in his day.

"I'd blow the whole shebang to hell – if it wasn't such a good cover," shouted the third man, brandishing his fist dramatically. He was tall and broad and straight for all his nearly seventy years. He wore a heavy trench-coat with brass grenade cleeks on the belt and a wide-brimmed American fedora hat. He looked like John Ford's idea of a Flying Column Commandant in the 'twenties – which might bear some relation to the fact that in the 'twenties he had been a touring actor specialising in the rôle of Robert Emmet.

His companion, the nose-clearing skeleton, who had commanded the Belfast Brigade in those days, said: "There's many's the Peeler that would face a machine-gun wouldn't dare put his neb into that kip."

"And I wouldn't blame him one bit," said the little man in the beret, who had been his Quartermaster, as they moved along the dark entry. "Protestant porter is bad enough, but at least it's Irish – and it keeps you regular. That English apple shit turns their insides to concrete. That's what has them blue in the face."

The others nodded gravely, as though in response to an invocation of the Deity: like all working-class Irishmen over sixty, after a lifetime of coarse cuisine, they equated the rhythm of life with the movement (or not) of the bowel.

They stopped in a deep gateway and the Quartermaster

tapped three times on the wicker. To a mumbled challenge from within he replied briefly in Irish and the gate opened to emit the sound of banjo music and a deep, nasal voice singing . . .

'The sun is burning in the sky,
Strands of cloud are slowly drifting by,
In the park the dreamy bees
Are droning in the flowers among the trees . . .'

Inside, the three men passed along the back of a hall at the far end of which was a stage of sorts. From there the singer scrubbed his banjo and told his sparse audience what would happen if the mushroom sun ever dawned . . .

'. . . Twisted sightless wrecks of men
Go groping in the dark and cry in pain . . .'

"Huh . . . sounds like 'The Devon Rooms'," muttered the Quartermaster, leading the way up a flight of stairs.

A young man in the audience, seated near the back of the hall with his girlfriend, happened to look round in time to see the trio passing through. He nudged the girlfriend, indicating, and whispered: ". . . If them oul' buggers got their hands on the Ultimate Deterrent they'd put it on a short fuse behind Hastings Street barracks."

* * * * * *

"Good-night, Anne-Marie."

"Good-night, Napper."

Good or bad, Napper was always there on Wednesday nights, his shoulder against the jamb of the door, his great bulk leaning cross-legged, a caryatid askew, almost filling the tiny hallway.

His was the third door up from her Mother's, and always the final giggle of the evening with her two younger sisters was when they spotted the glow of Napper's cigarette, waiting . . . "There's yer boy now, Anne-Marie. Better hurry or he'll get fractious." . . . "Seamus'll hear about it some of these days an' there'll be wigs on the green . . ." But neither they, Seamus nor anyone else knew what she and Napper knew. To them he was Napper the hard man, the ex-boxer who had gone to school with Anne-Marie and left it still unable to write his own name; to her Mother he was a shame and disgrace to the neighbourhood and the Church, bringing home to his sainted Mother's house that tinker's slut to pop out a child every year with the ease of a shelled pea and never do a hand's turn from one year's end to the next; to Seamus he was a lump whose reputation made him a useful presence on the door at a fund-raising hooley: but to Anne-Marie, Napper was her first love . . . .

It had happened during the summer holidays after their final year at school before she had gone on to the Big Nuns' and he'd signed on the dole. They'd spent the day playing, chasing, warring, in a crowd of others, up and down the back entry behind the houses, in and out of the backyards and through the bolt-holes in the adjoining walls that had been there since the Troubles in the 'twenties . . . a hot, dusty, sweaty day amid dust-bins and the accompanying blow-flies, mangy, irritable dogs and harassed, complaining Mothers. And at the end of it, in the warm dusk, Napper had taken her into the coalhole in his backyard, shut the door, and shown her what to do.

Until then she had had only the vaguest of notions. In her last year a wee nun had waxed briefly lyrical on pollination and the function of the bee and then lapsed into embarrassed silence. Her Mother, a holy woman deprived of that most holy of institutions, the double-figured family, had been going on about some other twelve-childered 'tinker' in the street and had put it all down to 'the drink'. Anne-Marie had noticed that when her Father came home on pay night with the smell of stout on him, he tended to break wind explosively, causing her Mother to chastise him for doing it in front of the children. All this, mixed up with the nun's wind-blown spores, had led Anne-Marie to suppose that humankind's method of random fertilisation was the common fart . . . Then, in the twilit coalhole, Napper had revealed his sting.

That first time, on hands and knees in the coal grit, had been painful in every way, Napper's knowledge of the ritual having been gleaned solely from observation of his Father's greyhounds. The second time, a week later on the floor of his parlour, had been less so, even pleasurable in an investigative sort of way. But the third and last time, behind a bush in the park after his first stretch in Approved School, had been horizontal and ecstatic. The memory could still make her tremble . . . Afterwards he had given her a ring, gold and scabbed with diamonds, which she had jettisoned down a manhole two weeks later, on the day he and another old schoolmate were sentenced to three years Borstal for a series of burglaries, one of which had been a jeweller's shop.

Napper had emerged from Borstal unrecognisable: huge,

scarred, surly and violent. By that time she was working in the
bank and going out with Seamus. When they passed in the street
Napper turned his face to the wall.

"Good-night, Anne-Marie."

"Good-night, Napper."

PAUL MULDOON

Three poems

The night before he was to be ordained
He packed a shirt and a safety razor
And started out for the middle of nowhere,
Back to the back of beyond,

Where all was forgiven and forgotten,
Or forgotten for a time. He would court
A childhood sweetheart.
He came into his uncle's fortune.

The years went by. He bought another farm of land.
His neighbours might give him a day
In the potatoes or barley.
He helped them with their tax demands.

There were children, who married
In their turn. His favourite grand-daughter
Would look out, one morning in January,
To find him in his armchair, in the yard.

It had snowed all night. There was a drift
As far as his chin, like an alb.
'Come in, my child. Come in, and bolt
The door behind you, for there's an awful draught.'

I am stretched out under the lean-to
Of an old tobacco-shed
On a farm in North Carolina.
A cardinal sings from the dogwood
For the love of marijuana.
His song goes over my head.
There is such splendour in the grass
I might be the picture of happiness.
Yet I am utterly bereft
Of the low hills, the open-ended sky,
The wave upon wave of pasture
Rolling in, and just as surely
Falling short of my bare feet.
Whatever is passing is passing me by.

I am with Raleigh, near the Atlantic,
Where we have built a stockade
Around our little colony.
Give him his scallop-shell of quiet,
His staff of faith to walk upon,
His scrip of joy, immortal diet –
We are some eighty souls
On whom Raleigh will hoist his sails.
He will return, years afterwards,
To wonder where and why
We might have altogether disappeared,
Only to glimpse us here and there
As one fair strand in her braid,
The blue in an Indian girl's dead eye.

I am stretched out under the lean-to
Of an old tobacco-shed
On a farm in North Carolina,
When someone or other, warm, naked,
Stirs within my own skeleton
And stands on tip-toe to look out
Over the horizon,
Through the zones, across the Ocean.
The cardinal sings from a redbud
For the love of one slender and shy,
The flight after flight of stairs
To her room in Bayswater,
The damson freckle on her throat
That I kissed when we kissed Goodbye.

BRAN

While he looks into the eyes of women
Who have let themselves go,
While they sigh and they moan
For pure joy,

He weeps for the boy on that small farm
Who takes an oatmeal Labrador
In his arms,
Who knows all there is of rapture.

Three poems

MORNING CALL

Up from the trawlers in the fishdock they walk to my house
On high-soled clogs, stepping like fillies back from a forge
Newly shod, to wake me at sunrise from a single bed
With laughter peeling skin from a dream ripening on the mossy
Branches of my head – "Let us in! Let us in!" – and half naked
I stumble over a floor of heaped paper to open my door of glass
To a flood that crosses the threshold, little blue waves

Nudging each other, dodging rocks they've got to leap over,
Freshening my brackish pools, to tell me of "O such a night
below in the boats!"."We can't go home! What *will* they say?"
Can I think of a lie to protect them from God only knows
What trouble this will cause, what rows? "We'll run away
And never come back!" – till they flop into black armchairs,
Two beautiful teenage girls from a tribe of tinkers,

Lovely as seals wet from fishing, hauled out on a rock
To dry their dark brown fur glinting with scales of salmon
When the spring tide ebbs. This is their everlasting day
Of being young. They bring to my room the sea's iodine odour
On a breeze of voices ruffling my calm as they comb their long
Hair tangled as weed in a rockpool beginning to settle clear.
Give me the sea-breath from your mouths to breathe a while!

With a lobster pot for a chair
    And a fishbox for a table
He'd sacrificed a plausible career
        On the London stage to live near
        The sea in a bare room
            Far from home
To become on the lips of islanders a fable.

        In an old pair of black jeans
        Threadbare though tautly darned
By himself needling with a woman's patience
        Buckled in a looted Hun's
        Eagle and swastika belt
            Disguised he felt
Reborn as a fisherman whose craft he learned.

        From an off-white Aran sweater
        Knit by his neighbour's wife
His dark face opened like a long love letter
        That makes a forlorn reader
        Revive with a gust of hope
            While he moused rope
For crayfish traps with a horn gutting knife.

        Through small panes of cobwebbed glass
        Across a limewashed stone sill
He hauled in shoals of riffled sun to please
        Only a few friends like us
        Because it was his style
            To play as well
Carrying a creel on his back or Coriolanus.

HUSBANDRY

Sheep like to graze on headlands
High up looking down on a raging sea.
It makes me dizzy to watch
An old ewe
Leaning over the edge to reach with her black mouth
A tuft of grass fine as hair.
I'd have to crawl there clutching frail stems.

How many of the flock fall
Dashed on to rocks or drowned in surf
To satisfy a peculiar hunger.
No soft herb
Pleases them as much as the spikes of gorse.
If I were their shepherd
I'd put them to fatten in a small safe paddock.

Prologue to

The Blue Macushla

a play

Time and place: 1970's, Dublin
Off, a piano is tinkling its jazz-blues arrangement of "Mother Macree". A desk lamp is focused on an empty chair; standing nearby, just discernible in the darkened office, two figures, one short, one tall, in trench-coats and hats: Vic Camden and The Bear; then the glow from a cigar betrays the presence of a third person seated on the other side of the desk: No. 1.
Off, in the night-club, desultory applause as the "Mother Macree" piece ends. Then Eddie's voice announcing:

EDDIE'S VOICE: Thank you, thank you! And now, folks, prepare yourselves to be transported, the star of our show – Star of the Galaxy – is going to sing a little number has a kinda special meaning for us here at the Blue Macushla. Take it away, Pete.
(The piano plays the introduction and "The Star of the Show" is heard singing "Macushla", in Marlene Deitrich style through the following)
Voices approach the office

MIKE'S VOICE: Yeah, three guys, boss.

EDDIE'S VOICE: And you let them in *where*?

MIKE'S VOICE: They said they wuz kinda associates.

EDDIE'S VOICE: You let them into my office?
(Eddie and Mike come into office, Eddie in tuxedo, Mike in doorman's uniform)

EDDIE: Okay, the house is full, you gotta book at least two weeks in advance . . . Hey, what's going on here? Mike,

	get these guys . . . (outa here)
	(The Bear has moved over behind Eddie and the gun in his pocket is sticking into Eddie's back).
VIC:	We don't need Mike, do we?
MIKE:	Boss?
VIC:	*(Slaps Mike's face with some paper money)*
	Be a good doorman, Mike, huh, and get back out there.
EDDIE:	Yeah, Mike, you get back on duty.
MIKE:	*(Accepting money from Vic)*
	Gee, thanks. Thanks.
	(Mike exits)
EDDIE:	. . . I sure am sorry, boys, but I can't do a thing unless you've got reservations.
VIC:	We just come from there, chief, for a pow-pow.
EDDIE:	Would someone mind telling me what this is all about?
NO. 1:	Please be seated, Mr. O'Hara.
EDDIE:	*(Attempting to assert himself).*
	Now hold on, this is my office, that's my chair you're sitting in.
VIC:	Sit, chief.
	(Eddie sits)
NO. 1:	You must forgive us for intruding on your privacy, Mr. O'Hara.
EDDIE:	Not at all.
NO. 1:	How good of you to say so. How little kindness is left in the world.
	(At a gesture from No. 1's cigar, The Bear places a parcel on the desk)
EDDIE:	Hey, what's that, whatcha got there?
NO. 1:	Show Mr. O'Hara what the package contains.
	(Bear unwraps the brown-paper parcel carefully)
EDDIE:	*(Frightened by the ordinariness of the contents)*
	What is it – what is it?
NO. 1:	Tell Mr. O'Hara what is it.
VIC:	That there, chief, is a pure $9 \times 4 \times 18$ inch carat concrete block.
NO. 1:	Now would you be so good as to tell me where you bank, Mr. O'Hara?
EDDIE:	Bank? I don't bank. This is a fun place, sure, but I've been having to borrow here, there and everywhere just to help it all along, see.
NO. 1:	Yes, quite, we know you borrow. Particularly from the Anderson Ryan Bank.
EDDIE:	Can't recollect I been in that one.

NO. 1:	Really? *(Passes a slip of paper to Eddie)* Perhaps this will jog your memory. It is a facsimile of a note left at the Anderson Ryan Banking Company Incorporated after business hours some six months ago.
EDDIE:	Yeah? What d'yeh know, how about that!
NO. 1:	Yes, how about it?
EDDIE:	You gonna let me in on what this is all about now?
NO. 1:	Thirty-five thousand pounds.
EDDIE:	Thirty-five thousand –? That's a lot of lettuce.
NO. 1:	We want the money, Mr. O'Hara.
EDDIE:	This is a joke! . . . – On my mother's grave! –
NO. 1:	I do not think your mother would be proud of your avowal. Show Mr. O'Hara how the concrete block works. *(The Bear lifts the concrete block to his eye-level, then drops it on the desk: Eddie pulls his hands away just in time).* You see? A very simple but effective invention. I am not a violent person, Mr. O'Hara, I abhor violence, but what am I to do in the face of such blatant untruths? Next time you may not be able to remove your fingers in time. After that, goodness knows where it may fall.
EDDIE:	I haven't got the money, I haven't got it! I'd got some bad debts here and every last nickel and dime was left after that also went into here. You gotta believe me!
NO. 1:	. . . I believe you, Mr. O'Hara. But, oh dear, what are we to do? We could inform the police, but the police do not look kindly upon us, so why should we aid them.
EDDIE:	Gimme time, I'll get it together, the club's beginning to really swing and –
NO. 1:	But we should then have to employ an accountant, Mr. O'Hara: inflation is running so high and all those calculations as to what should be an equitable rate of interest charged you: Oh dear! There are, of course, direct and conclusive measures which we ourselves can take against those who offend against us or in our name. But we are not an unreasonable order – we do not wish to kill Irishmen, though some will inevitably get killed, or executed, in the course of our campaign – and, where possible, we try to find a constructive solution for those who can find within themselves a sympathy for our work and a wish to further our ideals. Do you understand me, Mr. O'Hara? We should like to avail of the facilities your club has to offer from time to time. Well,

	don't just sit there, Mr. O'Hara, please say that you agree.
EDDIE:	Yeah, sure, yeah, I agree.
NO. 1:	How very good of you. Now let us introduce a little formality into the proceedings, the ceremonial of which will help you to keep in mind your obligation and the consequences of any default thereof. Please rise.
VIC:	Stand, chief.
NO. 1:	My friend.

(Vic raps the desk twice, formally)

By your own voluntary act you are now before us. Animated by love, duty and patriotism you have sought affiliation with us, and we have deemed you worthy of our confidence and friendship. We are Jsjtinfo, banded together for the purpose of freeing Jsfmboe, and elevating the position of the Jsjti race, and we shall hesitate at no sacrifice to achieve our aim. Are you willing to uphold the watchwords of our organisation: of secrecy, obedience and love? Answer yes or no.

| EDDIE: | Yeah – yes. |

(Two raps on the desk)

| NO. 1: | My friend, every man here has taken a solemn and binding oath to be faithful to the trust we repose in him. I assure you this oath does not conflict with any duty which you owe to God, to your country, to your neighbours, or to yourself. With this assurance will you now submit yourself to our rules and regulations and take our obligation without reservation? Answer yes or no. |
| EDDIE: | Yeah. |

(Two raps on the desk)

| NO. 1: | *(Hands Eddie a slip of paper)* Please take the oath. |
| EDDIE: | *(Reading)* My friends – |

(Two raps on desk)

I, number – number?

NO. 1:	Your number is nineteen, your division is T.
EDDIE:	I, number nineteen, local division T, do solemnly swear while life is left me to establish and defend a united Jsfmboe – What's this Jsfmboe?
NO. 1:	It is the code name of your country.
EDDIE:	That I will execute all orders coming from the proper authority to the best of my ability. That I will foster a spirit of unity, nationality and brotherly love among the entire people of Jsfmboe. I swear that I take the obliga-

tion without reservation, and that any violation hereof is infamous and merits the severest punishment.
Yeah.

NO. 1: So help you God.

EDDIE: So help me God.

(One rap on desk)

NO. 1: Brothers, it affords me great pleasure to introduce you to your new brother.

(Bear shakes hands with Eddie, wraps the concrete block and leaves. No. 1 follows. Vic shakes hands with Eddie)

VIC: Érin go bráth, chief, we'll be in touch.

(Vic leaves. Eddie gets a drink for himself, slumps into a chair, wonders what can he do. He gets a second drink for himself)

What it feels like to be a Writer

A talk for radio

I AM SOMETIMES ASKED – as, I suppose, all writers are sometimes asked – how I entered my career as a writer. I always answer that I did not choose this career; it was imposed on me by the gods. I was good for nothing else. And if you persist and ask me what is it exactly that made me "good" for writing and not "good" for anything else I would not know how to tell you. I have tried often to find out for myself why I am a writer and not, let us say, a painter or an actor or a musician or some other kind of artist, but I have never found a satisfactory answer. What would be the use of my saying that I was born imaginative, passionate, nervous, sensitive and so on? All artists have these natural advantages or disadvantages.

There are only two possible answers that make any sense to me. The first is that for as far back as I can remember I have never accepted that things are what they seem. I have always felt that everybody on earth goes about in disguise. So as a child, and to this day, my favourite myth or fable is *La Belle et la Bete* because the Beast was not what he seemed to be and the Beauty found out his truth by love. The other answer is that I have always understood things not with my brain but by means of dramatic images. This making of dramatic images is my only form of speech.

Lord Snow has recorded somewhere a story about two famous mathematicians which may explain what I mean by a "form of speech". One morning in 1913 in Cambridge University the first of those two men, whose name was G. H. Hardy, received in the post a big, untidy envelope with a lot of Indian stamps on it, containing some rather crumpled sheets of paper covered with line after line of fantastic looking mathematical theorems. They had been sent to him from Madras by a young man named Ramanujan, a poorly-paid and quite uneducated clerk. Hardy looked in boredom at those crazy-looking scribblings and threw them aside; but all that day they kept recurring to his mind and to make a long story short, he finally decided that they must be the work of a born mathematical genius. He brought Ramanujan to England to study, and in due course Ramanujan became a famous mathematician. He was made a Fellow of Trinity College, Cambridge and, at an early age, a Fellow of the Royal Society. Then, alas, he fell mortally ill. Shortly before he died, Hardy visited him in hospital, but since those two men had never talked about anything except mathematics, Hardy did not know what to say to his dying friend. At last, what he actually said was: "Ramanujan, I came here in a taxi. Its number was 1729. It seemed to me rather a dull number." At once the dying Ramanujan became quite excited. "No, Hardy!" he cried. "No, Hardy! That is a very interesting number. It is the smallest number that can be expressed as the sum of two cubes in two different ways." From that on they chatted away quite freely — presumably about numbers. The point of this story is that the gods had given these men at least one gift of speech. They saw life as numbers.

Because I can only speak in images, I see and describe the world as dramatic images. I invent people and I place them in certain situations or adventures. I throw them on the screen, as in a cinema: that is to say I throw them on a sheet of white paper; and my aim is to mesmerise my reader into believing that all those black scribbles on the page (like Ramanujan's mathematical theorems) are not just dots and letters but are real living people. More than that, my aim is to mesmerise the reader into believing that he is no longer himself but that he has become one of my characters. I make him identify himself with my characters. I aim to give him vicarious experiences, that is to say I give him the sensation of doing things that he may never have actually done himself. I make him live a new life. In short, I try to make him see life through my eyes. I am not saying anything original in all this. It is what all writers do. So when I read Thomas Mann's *The Magic Mountain* I think I am living in that sanatorium on that mountain. When I close the book I return to my own life – but my mind is by then coloured by images of aspects of life that I did not have before – the images of life of Thomas Mann.

When I was very young I had no images of life that I could call my own. I saw life only through other people's eyes. I read

The Three Musketeers and I at once saw all life as an heroic series of adventures. When I read novels or saw plays about the French Revolution or about Napoleon I also wanted to write novels and plays about 18th and 19th century France. I even persuaded myself that I had actually written novels about that period. When I was fourteen, I loved to tell my school-friends about a wonderful novelist named Jean François, and when I had finished telling them the story of the latest novel by Jean François, and they said, "That must be a wonderful novel, where can it be got?", I would draw myself up very proudly and say: "It can be got nowhere. I am Jean François. I am just finishing my novel."

In other words, I was not seeing life at all with my own eyes. I was seeing life only through the images or books of other writers. But this is how most writers begin – seeing life through other men's spectacles. It is very, very difficult for anybody to see life through his own eyes. In fact it is impossible until we have had enough experience of our own to force us to make up our own minds about what it is that we really are seeing. E. H. Gombrich put this strikingly in his wonderful book *Art and Illusion* when he said that most painters do not paint what they see – they see only what they are painting.

I will tell you very quickly about the experiences that made me see life through my own eyes. And they were, for me, very difficult and painful experiences indeed. I was born in a small provincial city in the south of Ireland before the first World War. What this means is that I was born in a country that at that time was part of the British Empire. I was educated in the English manner. I was being prepared to take my part in the life of the British Empire. I read world history as the English saw it. I read English literature as the English wrote it. All the boys' books and papers that I read were English boys' books and papers. For three hundred years, Irishmen had been moulded or melted into the English way of life by law, by brute force, by education. How could I see life clearly? I could not even see my own country clearly. I might just as well have been a boy born in Jamaica or Trinidad or India under British rule, unable to see Jamaica or India or Trinidad through any spectacles that had not been made in England. V. S. Naipaul's novel *The Mimic Men* depicts this process vividly. I might have been a boy born in Algeria under French rule, or an African boy born in one of the German colonies like Togoland or the Kamerun before 1919. It must have happened to countless subjects of the Roman Empire.

But it is impossible completely to crush the inborn spirit of an ancient people. There is always a minority that ancestrally remembers and longs and struggles for its lost freedom, say ten per cent or even twenty per cent of the population. And this minority always passes on to succeeding generations, even if it is only by word of mouth, the memories of the ancient greatness of the race. There is an amusing story about the attitude of certain Red Indians of America to a suggestion by President Johnson, during the Vietnam war, that the Americans might sooner or later leave Vietnam. A poll, or census, was taken in a certain Red Indian tribe to find out what they thought about this. Most voted, "Yes." But a minority of the tribe suggested that the Americans should also leave the United States.

I only very gradually discovered, through word of mouth, through little semi-outlawed papers published by a patriotic minority of rebellious Irishmen, that I was not English but Irish. I was sixteen years old when this extraordinary fact burst upon me like an explosion. That was the year 1916 when a handful of Irishmen rose in rebellion under arms against English rule in Dublin. They were, of course, defeated; a number of them were executed; but these executions pulled the brutal mask of Empire from the face of Ireland and revealed what Yeats called her "terrible beauty". They woke up the entire Irish people and the upshot of it was that after some six more years of fighting – like the long years of fighting in Algeria against France – the vast bulk of Irish men and women found themselves free.

Those six years were the years during which I got those personal experiences, of men and women, of politics and war, that at last helped me to see life through my own eyes – to make images of life that were both true to what I considered the secret reality of life, and true to what I considered, or hoped, was the secret reality of me: I was then aged twenty-two. I had, of course, been trying to write for years before then, but I had nothing much to write about until those six stormy years gave me appealing subjects. My first book of stories, dated 1933, was all about the revolutionary period. My first novel was a long autobiographical book about how an Irish boy, brought up in the English mode, begins to find personal freedom through the fight for freedom of all his people. Then I turned to another sort of freedom – the freedom a man may seek for inside his religion; which in Ireland means the Roman Catholic Church. That was called *Bird Alone*. And so, I have gone on writing ever since, saying my say about life as I see or think I see it.

Looking back, I realise that in everything I have written I have had but one thing to say about life as I see it. It is this: that life requires of each of us that we should grow up whole and entire as individual persons; that life is always trying to stop us from doing this; at the same time, that since the possibility is always there, we must fight on to the end for that freedom and wholeness of the Self.

So, in what I have written, I have tried again and again to make images of men or women succeeding or being defeated in this fight for wholeness. I have tried to image brief moments when some boy or man, girl or woman, does achieve perfection and happiness as a whole person, or just misses that perfect achievement. If they are foiled I always try to write with sympathy and understanding. I never pass judgment. I leave that to the reader.

I think one crucial thing that I have learned in a lifetime of writing is that we cannot love life, that is love other men and women, until we have first earned the right to love ourselves. Another thing I have learned is that although I have always a wary eye on life and on myself, I do not do this by arguing introspectively with myself – I do it by arguing with my characters on paper. It has always been my characters who have taught me anything I know about life or about me. I start by putting them down on paper to see how they will behave in some dramatic or testing situation. Quite often my character will, as I go along, reveal sides of himself and of life that I had never thought of when I began. This means that I often have to write my story several times, in several different ways, before I see him clearly. And at the end it is often this human fiction that I have created who creates himself, who reveals to me some truth that I had only partly guessed at when I began.

The only credit I take to myself in all this is that I at least have had the imagination and the sympathy to guess that every character, in every situation, contains a hidden truth that, if one works hard enough, if one presses him or her hard enough, will reveal itself when the last shred of conventional disguise falls at the story's end.

The Widow

an unfinished story

IN OUR VILLAGE THERE LIVED a peasant family named Talty. The
father of this family died young, leaving a widow and three
sons. The widow was of an unusual type and even in my time,
when she was quite old, in fact a hag, she had a countenance of
remarkable though savage beauty. Her cheeks were the colour of
the rose and her eyes were brighter than the sea at dawn. Her skin
was as smooth and as fresh as new milk. Yet her body was coarse,
like a mass of roughly moulded clay, with outstanding hips and
heavy legs. She moved heavily with a great raking stride. She was
stupid and superstitious. She always wore a frown of
unhappiness. Three sons were but a drop from the deep well of
her womb, that had been closed by her husband's death.

Among peasant women of her type child-bearing is a lust.
When thwarted, this lust becomes, by perversion, either greed or
sloth. At the time of their father's death, the sons were already
striplings and when the customary year of mourning had passed
and it was permissible for the widow to offer herself to suitors,
they were strong enough to deny her the right of giving them a
step-father. A step-father would rule in their house and govern the
land and produce children not of their blood, who might inherit
the fruits of their labours. So she remained a widow and became
the task-master of her sons, who had forced her womb to be
barren.

So it happened that although their land was counted poor
even in our barren village, this family grew prosperous. There
were thirty-two statute acres in their holding but at the time of the
father's death no more than nine acres were fertile. But the greed

of the widow and the young strength of the sons were proof against the poverty of nature. Like giants, these three striplings fell upon the rocks and tore them from their bed with crow-bars and sledge-hammers. They flattened mounds. They emptied the clay from deep holes with spades and carried it in baskets to the naked places. They gathered the earth from the roadsides and the sand from the sea-shore and they made fields where there had been barren crags. Before the eldest son had strong hairs on his jaws, the three sons had added ten fertile acres to their mother's land. They were the wonder of the village.

The people envied them and said they were no better than brutes of the wild forest. And indeed there was much truth in this jibe. Their house was on the western outskirts of the village, a little remote from the others. On one side of the western gable the great ocean lay eight hundred yards distant, visible through a gap between the cliffs. On the other side, the land sloped down to the calm sea that lay between the island and the mainland. So that in that house, between two seas, one thundering against the cliffs, the other murmuring sadly on the sandy shore, the nights were wild and haunted. And by day, the great bleak crag stretching to the west of the house, the common grazing ground of the village goats, that stood in groups, gazing in silence, made the place awesome. A great stone fence surrounded the house and a shaggy black dog guarded it from intruders. There were many outhouses and little gardens, all made by the sons, who worked about the house, building, when light had faded and it was no longer permitted by custom to work in the fields. And the villagers never visited the house, but went past with downcast heads and glanced furtively, as if there were something occult there.

Once only was something definite known in the village about the savage character of these three sons. A man called at the house to notify them that a bullock of theirs had jumped a fence, maddened by summer fever, and was wandering the roads. The three sons were having their mid-day meal when the man entered. A wooden form stood on the floor with its end to the fire. On the form there was a large kish filled with potatoes. In the centre of the kish was a plate of dried fish. The three sons sat around the kish, each with a knife. They had cut the fish into three portions. While the man was looking, one son trespassed with his fingers and tried to take a morsel of his brother's fish. Both struck at the back of his hand with their knives. Blood flowed out but the trespasser merely mumbled an oath and went on eating with his bloody hand. The mother sat on the hearth stool with potatoes and fish in her lap. And when the man delivered his message, they all looked at him sourly and one said that there was grass on the road. . . .

Three poems

ONE OF THEM

When one of them crossed the square
about dusk, tall, beautifully built,
the light of immortality shining in his eyes,
his black hair magnificently groomed,
passers-by would eye him, one
ask another if he knew him, if perhaps
he were a foreigner. The more attentive
marvelled, understood, stepped aside.
Then, just as he was lost from sight
under the arcades among the shadows
and the evening lights, headed
for that part of town
which comes alive only by night
in drinking and lasciviousness,
they would wonder which one of them
he might be, for what suspicious reason
he had come down into that street
from those august, venerated mansions.

after C. P. Cavafy

In principio
farmer, herdsman, fisherman,
one people over one Plain.
South the mountains' necklace,
the Caspian and Black Seas their jewel clasps.
Snowpeaks in sunshine.
Azure the spread sky.
Provocation for conquest.
Numerous as stones by the sea's shore,
the barrow grave mounds of my people
scatter the open Plain.
Sluggish the great rivers;
flex of their flood strength:
highways for transport,
migration.

Dark herds of cattle and horse
massed on wild grassland.

Uneasy the borders.

South stretch the lands of fair opportunity:
Dealers from cities and kingdoms
trek to our horse fairs
bringing metals and weapons and merchandise:
ornament bronze and dark woodwork
inlaid with ivory;
beaten bronze cauldrons for our religious rituals;
strong wine and dates and rich cloth lengths;
spices and incense
and jewelry to doll up our women.
We swap them horses,
to take their caravans home
and cotton and felt bales,
furskins and hides.

And most of our young men go with them as drivers,
stay on down south –
mostly as horsetrainers
but also as mercenaries when war's on,
joining on either side,

wherever the money or prospect of plunder looks better,
with cattle and horse raids and women
fringe benefits.

Southwards then I came . . .

WAITING FOR THE BARBARIANS

What are we all waiting for here in the public square?
    The barbarians arrive today.
Why is there so much lassitude in the Senate?
    How is it the Senators sit but pass no laws?
Because the barbarians are supposed to show up today,
    so, what laws should the Senators pass?
When the barbarians come, they will make the laws.
Why did the chief get up so early this morning?
    Why does he sit at the main gate
of the city, enthroned so solemnly, wearing his official insignia?
    The barbarians arrive today
    and the chief waits to welcome
    their leader. He's all prepared
    to present an official document
    inscribed with many titles, various names.
Why have our councillors and aldermen
paraded this morning all spit and polish
in their robes, carrying their staffs of office
so finely worked in silver and gold?
    Because the barbarians come today
and all this razzle-dazzle will impress them.
Why don't our great public speakers stand up
and make speeches as they always do?
    Because we expect the barbarians today
    and the barbarians have no time for eloquence.

Why this anxious bewilderment all of a sudden?
How serious people's faces have become!
Why are the streets and squares emptying so quickly?
Why is everyone going home again so upset?
    Because night has fallen
    and the barbarians have not come.
    Some travellers, arrived from the border,
    say there are no barbarians any more.
And now? Without the barbarians, what will become of us?
They were a kind of solution, those people.

                                                    after C. P. Cavafy

Three poems

INNÉ INNIU

Inné dúluachair
Inniu earrach
Tháinig chomh tobann
Le cat ag léim ar éan
Nó Billy The Kid ar a ghunna

Inné dúluachair
Inniu earrach
Tháinig chomh siuráilte
Le cíocha á gcruinniú i lámha
Nó fiacail a fháil amach

Inné dúluachair
Inniu earrach
Tháinig chomh ganfhiosúil
Le do ghrástúlacht rinceora
Nó ceol do shála im chluasa ag trasnú sráide

YESTERDAY TODAY

Yesterday in the grip of winter / Today spring / Came as suddenly / As a cat
jumping on a bird / Or Billy the Kid on the draw. / Yesterday in the grip of winter
/ Today spring / Came as surely / As breasts being rounded in one's hands / Or
having a tooth out. / Yesterday in the grip of water / Today spring / Came as
unknowingly / As your dancer's gracefulness / Or the music of your heels in my
ears crossing the street.

RINCE GRÉAGACH

Níl uaim ach a bheith leat
Go hard os cionn na cathrach
Balbhaíonn tú a bheith ann mé
Faid mo láimhe uaim
Is na hiarrachtaí chun a bheith
Smeairteáilte agus glic
Ni éiríonn leo
Ach éiríonn mo chroí
Nuair a chím an abhainn
Ag scaradh a géaga
Is ag teacht le chéile
Mar a dheineann do chorp ar ball
Ag rince Gréagach
Is do lámha i mo lámha-sa
Ag fuineadh cnámha a chéile
Is na focail alabastair go léir
Ina smidríní faoi do chosa rinceora
Ar an urlár fúinn

A GREEK DANCE

I only want to be with you / high up above this city / you being there leaves me speechless / an arm's length away / and the efforts at being / smartassed and clever / fall flat / but my heart rises / when I see the river / parting its limbs / and coming together / as your body does in a while / doing a Greek dance / and your hands in my hands / kneading each other's bones / and all the see-through words / in bits under your body's control / under your dancer's feet on the floor / underneath us.

FEARTLAOI FRANÇOIS VILLON
(ón bhFraincís)

A bhráithre a mhaireann inár ndiaidh
Ná tóg orainn ár ndíth-céille
Níl ionainn ach cúigear trúán
A fuair díol dlí daonna
Seo anseo crochta sinn
Gan ionainn ach na cnámha
Agus iadsan féin ag imeacht ina bpúdar
Tar éis an fhuadair go léir
Dheineamar béile do phréacháin
Ach guí chun Dé go maithfidh sé dúinne

Táimid marbh gan anam cráite
Impíg ar ár son trócaire
Ar Mhac na Maighdine Muire
A bhí riamh fial lena ghrásta
Is má daoradh sinn le ceart
An dtuillimid drochmheas
I measc ár mbráithre daonna
Tá's agaibh go maith
Nach stuama a bhíonn gach fear
Ach gur minic ina shaol dó gan aon splanc chéille

Nite agus sciomartha ag an mbáisteach
Loiscthe agus seirgthe ón ngréin
Dhá uaimh ar dhath an ghuail in áit na súl
Ár bhféasóga ár malaí ag an aer
Ní bhímid riamh aon am socair
Ach á luascadh gan staonadh ag an ngaoth
Mar seo nó mar siúd mar is maith leis
Níor pioctha ná méaracán ag na héin
Ná bígí mar sin páirteach lenár leithéidí
Ach guí chun Dé gach aon ní a mhaitheamh dúinne

L'EPITAPHE VILLON

Frères humains, qui après nous vivez, / N'ayez les cueurs contre nous endurcis, / Car, se pitié de nous povres avez, / Dieu en aura plus tost de vous mercis. / Vous nous voyez cy attachés cinq, six: / Quant de la chair, que trop avons nourrie, / Elle est pieça dévorée et pourrie, / Et nous, les os, devenons cendre et poudre / De nostre mal personne ne s'en rie; / Mais priez Dieu que tous nous vueille absoudre. / Se vous clamons, frères, pas n'en devez / Avoir desdain, quoi que fusmes occis / Par justice. Toutesfois, vous savez / Que tous les hommes n'ont pas bon sens assis; / Excusez nous, puisque sommes transis, / Envers le Fils de la Vierge Marie, / Que sa grâce ne soit pour nous tarie, / Nous préservant de l'infernale foudre. / Nous sommes morts, âme ne nous harie; / Mais priez Dieu que tous nous vueille absoudre. / La pluie nous a débués et lavés, / Et le soleil desséchés et noircis; / Pies, corbeaux, nous ont les yeux cavés, / Et arraché la barbe et les sourcils. / Jamais nul temps nous ne sommes assis; / Puis çà, puis là, comme le vent varie, / A son plaisir, sans cesser, nous charie, / Plus becquetés d'oiseaux que dés à coudre. / Ne soyez donc de nostre confrérie; / Mais priez Dieu que tous nous vueille absoudre.

Three poems

THE SLEEPWALKER

The wine-bottles in the rafters, eerily green,
Are lipped by cob-webs. Though the skylight throws
Its moonshine label crookedly across,
Their silence there is neither attic dream
Of cellar-ferment, faces leaning near
In banquet-glasses while the laughter grows,
Nor hope of ambrosia.

But alive in the ground-floor shadow of tables, chairs,
The eye of the kitchen storage-heater burns,
A point of fierceness.
The sleeping cat, the plant-pots on the sill,
The built-in cupboards, fluorescent lights,
Opaquely bedded in the ceiling-tiles
Will bask tomorrow in its afterglow.

He finds her on the landing outside their room
Where, mourning, she has missed the stairs that lead
Upwards or downwards and begins to turn
In corners of the alcove. Near a frame
The cold has jammed, a clouded net of pane,
She croons her broken, half-word sorrows;
Lost for the pressing darkness, out of reach
Of off-peak celebrations, the languid moon.

VII

Ashes of half-soles and stiletto heels,
     the blacks and blues
of straps and smouldering uppers;
     I am burning old shoes
on a bonfire in the garden,
     some of them yours:
everyday wear, the ornate, sad
     debris of the dancing years,
and bedroom slippers long trodden out of shape.
     Going up in smoke
with ancient, springless chairs that were not ours,
     the card-table someone broke
before we came here, tea-chests full of straw,
     they are acrid with the lives
that came to discard them,
     combustible as dead leaves.
No longer is it possible to tell
     which pairs we wore
walking at sunset in a loughside field
     that summer before
we travelled to terraces and pavement trees;
     or which embedded
the flattened pebbles of a country road,
     the grit that ached and faded
to less than pain or pearl of memory.
     Perhaps these helped to bear
the child inside you later when we trudged
     from one street to another with kitchenware
in suitcases and unpacked in larger rooms.
     We might have piled
our first bonfire then – the books you claimed
     had come between us – pulled
pages from spines, the bookshelf from the wall –
     except that we knew nothing is solved
so simply. So I am burning our old shoes
     eleven years on and we are still involved
in calms and crises, manageable flux,
     contentment and pleasure.
This task is neither sentimental rite

nor tedious chore; confidently insecure
I watch the dusty leather bubble and crack,
        the flames working
in grace and anger and flickering perfection
        towards garden earth, dark ashes in a ring.

THE SECURITY MAN

All through the sleety morning he keeps his body
    close to the heater,
its oil-blue flame the flickering subdued essence
of his emptiest hours.

A screen on a low table is showing repeats
of yesterday's programme,
stills of a wire cage outside a building,
cement in barrels.

So long has he watched, those might be the wet pavements
of a different city,
the images come to his elbow with dripping raincoats
a kind of surprise,

and they, reflexively, submit themselves
to his ritual patting,
their eyes across his shoulders already fixed
on the empty tables.

And that's it for the moment. It's been a year
since he mustered suspicion.
They have not looked at him and he has gone back
to supplementing his pension.

Four poems

1

Idir an tsúil agus eitilt na gcuach
Sreanga conasctha an cheatha
Ar a spléachann siad chugam a gcumha.

2

A cuid fabhraí –
Sreanga ar a suíonn fáinleoga
Sracfhéachaintí.

3

Osclaím vardrús m'aoise
Is fágaim d'ainmse istigh i ngach bliain ann
Mar liathróidí leamhan.

4

Piosaí poircealláin
Ag glioscarnaí sna caoráin –
Gealach i bplodáin.

1 Between the eye and the flight of cuckoos / the rain's connecting lines / on which they flash their sad farewells.
2 Her eyelashes – / wires on which sit the swallows / of glimpses.
3 I open the closet of my years / and into each of them, like moth balls / I insert your name, my dear.
4 Bits of china / glinting across boglands – / Moonpuddles.

COUNCIL ROOM

Three poems

English versions of poems in Irish

WHERE SHALL WE WALK?

Where shall we walk? The paths are all iced over,
On the grassy blankets of the roads we've known
Calcified mounds of slush and snow,
The wind stings the hollows of the knees
As slyly and as sharply as a whip . . .
I shall not walk with you. The flesh is stone.

We shall drive then, go to Mass,
Listen to *Hosanna in Excelsis*
Being ground out triumphally,
And feed upon the silly satisfaction
Of music swelling up the heart . . .
On a frosty day I act as chauffeur to the mysteries.

No, just no: I will not move today;
The chill has bloodied up my throat this long month past,
And every artery that makes a human burn
From brain down to the ground
Has been whitened to debility . . .
We'll wait and see if heat returns.

THE POET TO HIS WIFE

(From a three act play *Four Cheers for Cremation*)

A night of light persistent showers when I awake,
I turn towards you and see in wonderment
A stranger, motionless, laid out by my side,
And the animal within me leaps, for ecstasy.

But last night as thunder split the sky
(And the animal within cowed low in misery)
I said, 'If you, my wife this moment died
Shame would melt my heart and limbs.'
Today, of course, my reason jibs
At cosmic clichés of the kind.
A human being, I know, survives most things.

Yet, last night, my heart realized the melting shame
Of having kept you as a stranger in my territory,
Someone who after all those years I know much less
Than father, mother, brothers, relatives –
Who in this life exchange but words with me.
"Neglect like this" I told myself,
"Is bred out of barbarity."

But when the rumble in the sky had lost its potency,
And you my stranger wife beside me, soft and full of tenderness,
The animal in me leaped up again for ecstasy.

A GAELTACHT ROUSSEAU

Let her be, said the poet;
    do not chastise her,
she is still a stripling
and fear is a sickness
that stunts all human growth.

Let her be, said the poet;
do not chastise her,
let her grow unimpeded
to whatever height she is meant for:
the air is still soft above her head.

Three poems

BREACLACH

Gluaiseann na sluaite leo is fágann
Ina ndiaidh an fuíoll mar bhotún staire
Le aithrist ortha feasta i meon is i ngnás;
Clár a leasa, dar leo, a bheith dhá réir.
Breac áirithe é an fealsamh ar deoraíocht
Díleachta aimsire idir dhá cheann an mheá
Gan ceann faoi is fós gan tóigeáil a chinn
Ag scríobadh a scéil go ciúin i gcéir a anaim.

Ach b'fhéidir gur hiomaí sin babhta cheana
A scalladh gan choinne léas caol an léargais
Ar bhuilcín corr dítreabhach san Éigipt fadó,
Ar mhanach tuata thiar ag tóigeáil scrathógaí
Ar bhreaclach fhuar in Árainn nó Sceilig Mhíchíl.
Cá bhfios nar aimsigh snáthaid chaol an tsolais
An ceol úd ag seinnim i gcéir an n-anaim?
Scód go scriúta, sheol na sluaite leo.

STONEY PATCH

The crowds move on and leave / After them the remnants as history's blunder /
To mimic them in mind and manner; / Their welfare, they say, to be as them. /
A peculiar fish is the philosopher in exile / An orphan of time in the balance /
Without bowed head or yet head on high / Scratching his story in the wax of
his soul. / But maybe many's the time before / The thin beam of insight was
flashed out of the blue / On some odd posse of hermits in Egypt long ago, / On a
laymonk gathering dungcakes in the west / On a cold stoney patch in Aran or
Skellig Rock. / How can we know the fine needle of light didn't catch / In their
soul's wax that music playing? / Sheet to shroud, the crowds sailed on.

Lomchnáimh na fírinne é
Gur fuar do thóir ar nuaíocht
Milliún uair nó dhó ó shin
Tharla an t-iomlán romhat.

Céard eile atá againn le rá –
An t-iomlán dearg a tharla;
Anseo ar nós páiste spréachta
Réabann muid an bréagán féin.

Céard atá ann ach deideighe –
Goideann an draíocht ón bhfírinne,
Cluifeálann an teas ón bhfuacht,
Bris sa dorchadas é an·solas.

Diúgaireacht is ansa linn
An banrán anois an phaidir
Maoin an tsinsir i bhásta
An oidhreacht againn le meath.

'Sé an domblas deiridh é
An leide féin a chailleadh
Gur dhúinne atá ag tarlú
Gach is ar tharla romhainn.

TEARING

It is the bare bone of truth / Your search for news is vain / A million times or two ago / The whole happened before you. / What else have we to say – / The whole caboodle happened; / Here like a crazed child / We tear the toy itself. What is it only a bauble – / Magic steals from truth / Heat filches from cold, / Light is a loss for heat. / The whine to us is dearest / The grumble now the prayer / The patrimony to waste / The legacy for us to dissipate. / It is the last bitterness / To lose the inkling itself / That it is for us is happening / All that happened before.

Cleasaí sorcais é gabhalscartha
  Ar a dhá bheithíoch marcaíocht
Eachaín ghiongach na daonacht,
Capall dodamach na hoibre.

Dingliseach an ealaíon í in airde
Timpeall ina bhogshodar leo
Ceachtar acu ní hansa leis
Faitíos aon scaoll a chur iontu.

'Mise an nádúr, mise an gean
Lig liomsa,' arsa an eachaín,
'Mar ús iolraidh rathaímse
Raithneach nó clann clainne.'

'Muise, éist léi,' adeir an capall
'Liomsa sodar sásta na hoibre
Liomsa an staidéar, an gaisce
Is slat tomhais don aimsir.'

Buailtear bosa don chleasaí
Timpeall ina bhogshodar leis
I gcois dá leith ar an aoibhneas
Marach an scroig san adhastar.

CIRCUS

He is a circus astride / Two mounts / The restive steed of human kind-ness, / The jibbing workhorse. / It is a ticklish business aloft / Around in an easy trot they go / Neither dearer to him / Fearing to panic them. / 'I am nature, I am love; / Give me rein,' says the steed,/ 'Like compound interest I thrive / Bracken or childrens' children.' / 'Oh listen to her,' says the horse / 'Mine is work's contented trot / Mine the thought and feat / Which is the yardstick of time.' / Applause for the artist / Around in an easy trot he goes / Straddling the joy / But for the fray in the halter.

Two scenes from

Catchpenny Twist

a charade

Bookshop

Martyn is looking through some poetry collections. Marie enters.

MARIE: Surprise.

MARTYN: Marie!

MARIE: So this is where you've run to?

MARTYN: What are you doing here?

MARIE: Visiting friends. Selling books. What about you? Here. (*She gives him a* Sinn Féin *pamphlet from her satchel.*) Thirty pence, please.

MARTYN: Roy and me are getting established, with the songs. We've got a couple of records out, with Monagh. We're doing an entry for Eurovision at the minute. Listen, I'm sorry about the ballad. We had to leave Belfast in a bit of a rush.

MARIE: Very wise. I'm surprised at what's become of you, Semple.

MARTYN: Me?

MARIE: Fletcher always was a wee Orange pimp, under the skin.

MARTYN: Easy on, Marie.

MARIE: You're in his pocket, that's the thing. I thought you told me your grandfather carried a gun in the 'twenties.

MARTYN: The past is over and done with, Marie. We're in the Common Market now.

MARIE: You amuse me.

MARTYN: Men have been on the moon. It's a small world.

MARIE: Don't delude yourself, you can't just turn your back on generations of the dead. Don't imagine you'll get away with it that easy.

MARTYN: I'm in favour of a united Ireland as much as the next man.

MARIE: What are you doing reproducing this pseudo-American slop, then?

MARTYN: What? What has that got to do with it?

MARIE: Everything, that's all. The whole state apparatus of this country, North and South, is designed for one function – sell out. Selling out the resources, the heritage, the culture, the very soil itself to foreign speculators.

MARTYN: Come off it.

MARIE: You're a cog in that machine, you and your Common Market and your Eurovision Song Contest.

MARTYN: For God's sake, Marie, that's completely wired up. I mean, people enjoying songs, a harmless entertainment . . .

MARIE: Nothing that mediocre is ever harmless.

MARTYN: You've lost touch with real life.

MARIE: You've lost touch with who and what and where you are. Don't think you can escape for ever into mass-produced catchpenny idiocies.

MARTYN: Pop songs are like the folk music of our generation. There's nothing political about it.

MARIE: That's really rich, coming from you, in your position.

MARTYN: What are you talking about?

MARIE: I'm talking about why you did a flit.

MARTYN: Somebody posted bullets to us.

MARIE: You're damn lucky they didn't arrive at a higher velocity.

MARTYN: Why do you say that?

MARIE: Considering what you were mixed up in.

MARTYN: Us? We'd no involvement in politics whatsoever as you know.

MARIE: Don't act all innocent. You took to the wing the minute it appeared in print.

MARTYN: Whatever you're on about, Marie . . . I think maybe I'd rather not know.

MARIE: You're not bluffing, are you – you really don't know what you've got yourself into. There was an article in a Protestant paper. Naming you two. It said you'd both been supplying entertainment to their drinking clubs. As a means of gaining information about them. On behalf of the British Army. The proof was that you were also doing work for the I.R.A. You're in dead trouble, Martyn.

MARTYN: But none of it's true!

MARIE:	Oh? You did no work for the Protestants, then?
MARTYN:	We wrote a few comedy numbers for a cousin of Roy's, that's all.
MARIE:	You're the original babes in the wood, aren't you?
MARTYN:	What'll happen? What should we do?
MARIE:	These things aren't forgotten.
MARTYN:	We literally didn't know. I suppose there's no point in even trying to refute it now.
MARIE:	Not much.
MARTYN:	Good God, Marie, surely you never believed it?
MARIE:	I wouldn't put anything past Fletcher, but I was sceptical all the same. Even the Brits have more gumption than to employ the likes of you.
MARTYN:	I can't get over it.
MARIE:	Well, the best of British luck, as they say. I hope it's got more to offer than British justice.
	(She makes to leave)
MARTYN:	Don't run off – what about a drink?
MARIE:	Sorry – I've another three shops to go round.
MARTYN:	See that girl over there?
MARIE:	What about her?
MARTYN:	Just before you came in, she shouts up to the woman at the cash register – Audrey . . . where the hell's *The Savage Mind*? I thought it would make a beautiful skit. Two assistants shouting across the heads of the customers – Where's *The Female Eunuch*? I don't know, but there's a couple of Trollopes under the counter . . . *(She smiles)* You remember the old college revues?
MARIE:	Of course I do, why wouldn't I?
MARTYN:	You were some stage manager.
MARIE:	You were some comedian.
MARTYN:	We put in a lot of happy days and nights together, Marie.
MARIE:	It was half a lifetime ago.
MARTYN:	Seven years, that's all.
MARIE:	Some seven years.
MARTYN:	It's tragic to let is just completely vanish, all the same.
MARIE:	You have to grow up sometime, Martyn.
MARTYN:	You've time for a quick jar, come on.
MARIE:	No, I'm away. Incidentally, the Irish History section's over there.

She leaves. Martyn, left alone, tears the pamphlet in half. Blackout.

* * * *

Marie Kyle has entered a pub with a girl, as a friend, in tow

MARTYN: Hello, Marie.

MARIE: You'd swear there was one of us following the other.

MARTYN: What brings you here?

MARIE: We've been doing a radio programme.

ROY: I thought your crowd was banned from the air.

MARIE: An Irish language programme. So far as I know we're still allowed to breathe the air.

ROY: It's a pity you don't extend that right to your victims.

MARTYN: *(Hastily):* Monagh's just been recording one of our numbers for a radio show.

MARIE: Children's Hour, is it?

ROY: She's doing another prison concert next week, with a bit of luck you'll be able to attend it.

MARTYN: Listen. We used to be good chums. The four of us. The old college gang.

MARIE: Where have you been for the last seven years? The country's been at war, you know, a lot of chums are in prison. A lot of chums of mine have given their lives.

MARTYN: The thing of it is – Roy and I just aren't politically involved.

ROY: We don't swallow the sort of fanatical gunk that you use to justify murder.

MARIE: I know where I stand. On eight hundred years of history, eight hundred years of repression, exploitation and attempted genocide . . .

ROY: I live in the twentieth century, love.

MARIE: . . . this time we're going to put an end to that for all time. There's unfinished business in this country . . .

ROY: You know, the twentieth century – aeroplanes, spin dryers. Pinball machines.

MARIE: . . . and you're involved as much as any other Irishman which is right up over your ears whether you want to be or not.

ROY: You can keep your history. You belong in it. They should build museums for you instead of prisons. The rest of us want shot of it. *(To Martyn)* Let's go. *(He leaves)*

MARTYN: I mean, we could still be friends, without having to agree about all this. We used to just discuss it over a beer.

MARIE: You're both like two spoiled brats! Irresponsible children!

MARTYN: *(Going):* You've let yourself get bitter, Marie.
        (He leaves)
MARIE: *(Shouting after them):* There's fifteen thousand British troops fighting an imperialist war on the soil of your own country! When are you going to wake up? What are you going to do about it?

Desertmartin

a poem

At noon, in the dead centre of a faith,
  Between Draperstown and Magherafelt,
This bitter village shows the flag
In a dry absolute September light.
Here, the Word has withered to a few
Parched certainties, and the charred stubble
Tightens like a black belt, a crop of bibles.

Because this is the territory of the Law
I drive across it with a powerless knowledge –
The owl of Minerva in a hired car.
A Jock squaddy glances down the street
And grins, happy and expendable,
Like a brass cartridge. He is a useful thing,
Almost at home, and yet not quite, not quite.

It's a limed nest, this place. I see a plain
Presbyterian grace sour, then harden,
As a free strenuous spirit changes
To a servile defiance that whines and shrieks
For the bondage of the letter: it shouts
For the Big Man to lead his wee people
To a clean white prison, their scorched tomorrow.

Masculine Islam, the rule of the Just,
Egyptian sand dunes and geometry,
A theology of rifle-butts and executions:
These are the places where the spirit dies.
And now, in Desertmartin's sandy light,
I see a culture of twigs and bird-shit
Waving a gaudy flag it loves and curses.

from a novel in progress
Ferris Moore

FERRIS MOORE IN THE UNLIT ROOM stared through the window at the approaching night. The fields were all silver and shade, the mountains great, black masses. Above them shafts of pale yellow light were merging into grey. Above them too, small, black clouds in ragged line on line moved steadily and endlessly, a great army bent on the super-terrestrial business of Someone or Something beyond the apprehension of Ferris Moore and his humble fellows, purposeful nuncios of the wind and of that Something or Other's command and will. The window framed it all and the wind, which made a noise about the house, tossed the trees and scattered the leaves. The wind, he knew, was cold and the roads winding high into the mountains were flanked by tormented heather and bracken.

He thought of a boy and his companions descending from those hills on such an evening long years ago, a boy with calf muscles grown stiff from effort and the sweat on his back grown cold and the chill smell of canvas and rubber rising from his cape and haversack. A lifetime ago. Several lifetimes ago, if such were possible. He thought so.

The world was very beautiful; cold, lonely, comfortless, uncaring yes – but beautiful. Nature was an unending display of sublime virtuosity, in which shape and movement and colour and combination echoed at times, and at other times mocked, the soul's intimations of immortality. Wordsworth had found it so. Then why not Ferris Moore? It was an immortality not necessarily accessible to the soul of Ferris Moore. In all likelihood an immortality away and beyond the soul of Ferris Moore. An immortality nevertheless (he acknowledged the fact on certain rare occasions) coveted by It.

O my poor soul, Ferris Moore thought, why do you trouble yourself? Why look with such longing and heartbreak on the casual and unregardworthy glories of some mindless accident? Because (Ferris Moore answered himself, as he sometimes did) they are the only fit symbols of the aspirations, the laughter, the kingliness, the brotherhood, the heartbreak that this lowly clod of earth by some miracle of grace has encompassed. That, and not for the first time, puzzled him.

He left the window. He lit the lamps. He drew the curtains.

from

Down all the Days

an adaptation of the novel by

CHRISTY BROWN

Act 2 Scene 5. The street. Father enters carrying a brown paper parcel and a naggin of whiskey in his hand. He reels, as much from the habitual pain in his head as from alcohol.

FATHER: Night, Magso, night, Essie. And to you woman of the house, me darling Alanna, adieu. And hear this, I'll have that slate cleaned, scrubbed, before you've time to bless yourself. *(Pause. He raises his hand demonstratively)* My apologies, my heart-felt apologies. I should have known, I should have known by that quaint Northern brogue that you could be of the other persuasion. Now, there's nothing very seriously wrong with you in my book if you happen to be born a few miles the wrong side of the border. I hold no grudges. I fought in the war of Independence meself. I fought for the green, white and the orange. And I'm not going to say another word on the matter, not another word. I'm just going to say goodnight, God bless, and don't worry about that slate 'cos it'll be scrubbed clean before you've time to add it up. *(He moves off)* Not much of a pub. Pouting me lungs out for them night after night, week after week. Keeping the bloody place alive. Oh, they know me strength all right. They know I'll pay up. Slate as long as a countryman's mile. Wipe it out, scrub it, gone. The curse. *(He looks up. Sees something. Blesses himself)* Good God, blessing meself passing a Protestant

	Church. That's where your man ended his days . . . Swift.
	That's it, Swift.
NARRATOR:	Dean . . . the mad Dean.
FATHER:	Still, not much of a pub.
NARRATOR:	He founded a hospital for the alcoholics of Dublin town.
FATHER:	Decent man, the Dean, but I'm no alco. An educated
	drinker, that's me.
NARRATOR:	Time up, time up long ago.
	(A loud bell sounds. Father puts his hands to his head)
FATHER:	Jesus, there's a time bomb exploding in me head. *(Bell*
	sounds again) Somebody tell that Dean to control his iron
	fist or I'll bleedin' tear down his tower around me. Smash
	it with the bleedin' hammers in me head, I will. *(The bell*
	sounds again)
NARRATOR:	Somebody has to keep time.
FATHER:	It's rattling in me head. Murder, that's what it's rattling.
NARRATOR:	How many more hours have you left, it's asking, how
	many more hours?
FATHER:	Who's bothered about dying? Not me. I'm not worried
	about me exit. They can deposit me where they like. An
	unmarked grave in the bloody wilds for all I care. I'm not
	worrying. What's a hole. A hole is . . . a hole.
NARRATOR:	Black gaping sore in the earth.
FATHER:	It's a trapdoor. An escape. Sure, every man needs one.
	(Looks to his hands) Maggots have to live too. And it
	doesn't matter to them where they dig your hole. They get
	you in the end. *(Final bell. He looks up)* Never a day sick in
	me life. They can't take that away from me. Chime out me
	sins but you can't take that away . . . Can you say as much
	for the young men of today? Women, that's all they think
	about. The opening between the thighs.
NARRATOR:	Gateway to paradise.
FATHER:	Moy ah. They won't earn their keep in heaven that way.
	Christ, if they knew what they were letting themselves in
	for they'd let the poor bloody cock sleep. *(Pause)* But look
	at them. Look at the half light, the hallways. The animals.
	In front of the kids and all. Jesus, in my day . . .
NARRATOR:	In your day a man couldn't kiss a girl in public without
	someone running for the priest.
FATHER:	The priest would have beat the fear of God into the little
	buggers in my time. *(He looks all around)* Not a street
	lamp-post for miles to flush the fornicators out.
NARRATOR:	It's these tenements breed corruption.

FATHER: The Corporation never did anything right, again.
NARRATOR: Again?
FATHER: Them bombs on the far off North Strand. No need to go to London now, me boy. Or to that other war that never ends.
NARRATOR: On the home front.
FATHER: Domestic warfare. I'm weary of it. *(Takes a slug from the whiskey bottle)* The false amber escape route. Never a day sick in me life. Up with the lark every morning, no matter what. Can't take that away from me, can they? The young fornicators of today, can they boast as much? Hot bloody stallions, that's all they are. Give them a couple of pints and they're dead men. Not like their fathers. *(Drinks again)* Begetting bloody kids who puke on the sweat and toil it takes to put food in their bellies and the fear of God into their mean little hearts. Kids . . . thank God the missus is past all that. Just an empty sack now. Dive in as often as I like now. No little fishes swimming in the dark pool now. Jesus, if I'd known when I was pumping it out what I was letting meself in for, I'd have tied a bloody knot in it. The casual, feckless way they just keep on multiplying. Like rabbits. As bloody regular as winter cold. Bloody unfair on me. I didn't part the whiskers too often, did I? Jesus Christ, what's a man made for if not for that. Up the pole with you me good woman, up the pole with you and no hemming or hawing about it. This is the way the poor people live and it's marked down on the slate. God marks it down every time. Every time I gave her a child he marked it down in me favour. *(Pause)* No I never knew what I was letting meself in for. Wouldn't have held back though, even if I had. Would have had to kill me, or castrate me. Felt the need, no matter how tired, or jaded. And nothing better in this wide and weary world, God knows, than the soft things of a woman. And a good enough woman she was once. None better in her day. Small and firm and tight, till the kids came along. Promise of the morning; that's what she was. Till she put on the spread. A flower she was, at the beginning, opening petal be petal, open to the world but only for me.
NARRATOR: Don't be seeing that drunken bowsie, that Whelan fella.
FATHER: Picnics out on the broad acres of Broadstone.
NARRATOR: He'll drag you into the gutter, along with himself.
FATHER: Pricked her finger on a thorn and I sucked her warm blood.

NARRATOR: Are you out of your mind going out with the likes of that cornerboy?

FATHER: I felt bloody foolish in me Fianna Eireann uniform and she in her fine black lace mantilla.

NARRATOR: What would your poor dead mother say?

FATHER: I felt afraid. Only wanted to play cards with the rest of the lads. Not break down the walls of this jaunty little Jericho of a town. Yet for her, for her I'd have faced the whole murderous gang of Black and Tans single handed.

NARRATOR: You fought for your country, for bloody Sinn Féin.

FATHER: I fought for her, me child bride, barred from me be wrinkled old aunts and uncles who wanted her to marry the clean mannered gentleman from Irishtown, that's who I fought for.

NARRATOR: And she bore you her litter. The last shakings of the bag, that last kid. You can empty yourself into the garbage can now, when you can.

FATHER: And me, what about me? Sucked dry I am. Drained like an ould orange. That's something women don't understand. They think it's just a question of putting it in and taking it out. It's not that bloody simple. It's not just that you put it in. It's something else. Something deeper.

NARRATOR: Adam's rib.

FATHER: Each one that came bawling out took a part of me with them. Making me less. Weaker and weaker. Me heart's blood, that's what I poured in.

NARRATOR: And all that remains is a shroud of skin upon a frame, bending and shaking in the wind like a scarecrow.

FATHER: Sweet suffering God, the time I was renovating that house down on the quays. The nest of baby mice they put in me lunch box. I felt bloody sick, just looking at them . . . little raw pink things . . . no eyes, no mouths, just lumps of boneless raw flesh. What did that bastard think he was up to putting twins into her? Didn't he know she was too bloody skinny. Must be a mistake. Poor bloody her . . . poor bloody me, poor bloody people . . .
(The bag slips from father's hand. He makes to retrieve it, slips and falls.)

NARRATOR: And he carries his pack, but the hammers inside his skull crucify him.
(Enter Marg dressed as a teenager)

MARG: Are you all right, mister?

FATHER: Dear thorny headed Christ, how did I get down here?

MARG: What's wrong, mister?

FATHER:	Marg . . . is that you Marg? Help me for Christ's sake.
MARG:	I'm not Marg, mister, but I'll help you.
	(She struggles to pull him up. A policeman enters)
MARG:	Hurry, mister, there's a rozzer coming.
POLICEMAN:	Everything all right, miss?
MARG:	Just me Da. I'm taking him home.
POLICEMAN:	I can phone for the squad car if you like.
MARG:	No thanks, I'll manage him. Come on, Da, we're nearly home.
	(Policeman looks on the smashed bottles on the ground. Marg sweeps them aside with her foot).
MARG:	Out of harm's way.
POLICEMAN:	Sure you can manage now?
MARG:	Positive sure, sir.
POLICEMAN:	Good night so.
	(He moves off)

The Conservative

I

Time now to consider knickers,
frail gaudy triangles stretched
rich-textured as rope
in close-up on soft alps,
your alabaster bum.
                    Ah!
but your smile hardens.

            I am wrong.
I admit. Apparently glad rags
are not intended to tempt me
but to keep you warm. I laugh
but I'm not mocking!

                Use
your historical imagination.

In my day, my other days,
suspenders, stockings, slips, etcetera,
were paradisal accoutrements
to be gained, regained.

Holding my mother's hand
in a shop in Ferryquay Street
where she bought thread, my glazed
eyes caressed the glossy card
on the counter, the Kaysar Bondar girl
whose impossibly long dark legs
receded into clouds of underclothes
and a hard struggled in my schoolboy
shorts for recognition.

Go easy, love,
on a reformed old sexist, his agonies
of withdrawal, the long effort. Imagine
for instance one of those spruce and hollow
ex-alcoholics waking one morning
alone in a well-stocked bar who once
had begged and forced entry in the old
days of fierce addiction. To find it
all free and available and not to be touched!

"No, never touch it, thank you." Oh,
the injustice! If only
I'd had you in my prime.

II

I am willing to learn, love,
but you must be able
to tell the intrinsic
from the fashionable.
It was no chauvinist
but a connoisseur
sighed as your bra hit the floor
carelessly, and your knickers
were off in a sweep inside your jeans.
You were wrong to cheat your lover
of such sweet scenes.

If this is liberty
to fuck and be fucked
in puritan simplicity,
I am a counter-revolutionary.

Christians, who eat their god,
even, find It repetitive
lacking music and ritual.
Call me conservative –
but imagination and style
matter. You offer yourself – wow! –
and I will kneel and devour
my darling; but it matters how.

III

A nd this can be only beginning.

Under my banner will throng together
the rhyming poets and audible singers,
drummers with cymbal and brush, and bands
you can hear yourself talk above!

When the female string trios
arise from behind their potted
ferns the future is mine!

Oh, join me in that ecstasy
and I'll instruct you personally
in slow-foxtrots, in holding hands,
in sitting on knees. What could you want
more? . . . ordering cakes and teas
at Forster's Family Restaurant
where old-style waitresses in black
will teeter forward and teeter back
with the heavy silver service,
armoured in starched aprons
and unfailing servility.

Back. Back. Back.
Let us follow my longings
to a Donegal again thronging
with faithful maids, and nannies
as sensual and superstitious
as John Hewitt's or Forrest Reid's
Or Louis MacNeice's.

Remember that awful telephone call
ending an era, when Mrs. Boal
stiffened, hoping she was mistaken,
and a faint voice from St. Johnston repeated
(and obviously drink taken),
"There are no maids left in Donegal."

IV

When your old conservative dies
before you, dry your blue eyes.

Imagine me busy as usual
maybe in limbo, gathering
lost babies who died for causes
long forgotten since,
aborted by hot baths and gin
in sordid lodgings, aborted
in modern clinics under control,
hygienically done in.

The true conservative regrets
all loss, even dispersed semen
your soft mouth swallowed or spat
out, that I glimpsed smeared
on our glowing bellies, heaving
in ecstasy, being rubbed away,
evaporating, or trapped
in those feather-light bags
we knotted so cheerfully
that lay all night at the bedside.

Even the eggs that descended regularly
once a month in your womb out of oblivion
to keep their appointment, waifs
waiting for days (tell them we came,
that we kept the faith) drifting away.

V

If drop-out students
could drop in, then,
if forsaken girls and former
wives could be only
embraced again and explained to,
then usefully I could
wait out that interim,
as I wait for you now,
to hear your laugh, unlady-like
behind me, the clink
of the half-bottle of whisky
or other strong drink,
your astounding cool arms
again interrupting my work,
your hair surrounding me.

But maybe it's not on.
Particular beauties may have to go
along with our bad habits.
The Provos may not know
themselves from the Stickies,
if in eternity no one bickers
over old hurtful distinctions,
if nothing that mattered matters
and nobody wears knickers.

from

The High Consistory

a novel

O NE EVENING IN THE EARLY AUTUMN of 1922 he took the boat to
Liverpool with a bundle of notes, a sheet headed *Oglaig
na Eireann* followed, in brackets, by 'The Irish Volunteers'
and a typed shopping list for specific types of small arms. The
idea of carrying the money and documents anywhere but in his
jacket pocket did not occur to him.

The civil war was a few months old and Simeon, partly
because of his air of youthful gaucherie, his Australian passport
and his being uninvolved in previous armed activity, had been
asked by the commander of a country column, then lying
wounded in a house in Dublin, to undertake the mission.

With his two smart-looking, almost empty suitcases, only one
of which he himself was to return with fully packed, he took a
train across the grimy English midlands to Hull.

As he sailed down the Humber estuary on a ship bound for
Ostend with late holiday makers, he sought out the Purser; not on
a sudden impulse but driven by a compulsion that had been at the
fringe of his consciousness (never fully acknowledged) ever since
he had agreed to the trip. Was it, he wondered, one of those crazy
but necessary impulses (necessary to a pattern he couldn't
decipher) that at times possessed him and that had been behind his
ridiculously early and hurried marriage?

The bearded sailor in braided uniform was helpful and
unexpectedly sympathetic, perhaps welcoming a change from the
usual tourist enquiries. He consulted a directory in his tiny office
and gave Simeon an address in Brussels of a trade mission rather
than a consulate, which Simeon, thanking him, stowed away with

the rest in his inside pocket. He was still uncommitted.

When, however, the train from Ostend stopped at Ghent (Gand), instead of alighting on the platform that smelt of cigars, he closed his eyes and sat back in his corner seat. In Brussels he left the cases at the station and took a taxi to the address in the rue de l'Ecuyer.

After a wait in an anteroom, he was taken into an office whose walls were covered with posters depicting industrial scenes in the Soviet Union, that had captions in French and Russian. A frozen-faced official at a desk listened to Simeon's explanation, in a mixture of French and English and showed no sign of understanding either, but let him continue to the end, at which point a young woman from another desk butted in. In a French that Simeon understood fairly well, indicating, he thought, that it wasn't her native tongue, she mentioned somebody called Elsa Triolet whom she was going to telephone in Paris. Leaving him with a volume of English translations of poems by Esenin and Mayakovsky, she then left the room.

He supposed that she'd mentioned the name of her friend in Paris whom she'd no doubt an appointment to phone at a stated time, so that he should not think she'd gone off in the hope that her stern-faced colleague would get rid of him, or at least to let him cool his heels, as they say, and rethink his preposterous request.

When she returned, though, she told him that she hadn't been able to get hold of the mysterious Elsa who, as he may not have heard, had recently left her husband, M. Triolet, but that he needn't worry on that account (on which account? Surely not about the separation of a couple of whom he'd first heard ten minutes ago? Presumably about the helpful young woman's failure to contact her). She had heard that Mayakovsky was at this very time in Berlin with Elsa's sister, where she wouldn't be at all surprised if Elsa hadn't joined them, though her informant (the unhappy M. Triolet? but there was no use his trying to guess when he was so out of his depth) hadn't said so.

She gave him the name of the hotel where the famous young Russian was staying. All he had to do now was to obtain an authorisation from the Allied Occupation Commission to pass through their zone in Germany and possibly a German visa, of that she wasn't sure.

All went unexpectedly smoothly, though getting the stamps on his passport delayed him in Brussels a couple of days. On the evening of the third he arrived at the Bahnhof-am-Zoo in Berlin and took a taxi straight to the address he'd been given.

Simeon was somewhat disappointed at the look of the hotel and of the street in which it was situated, but for all he knew, the great Russian revolutionary might not wish to draw attention to himself by appearing in one of the grander places. Or indeed, he had just thought of that, it might be in accord with Soviet principles.

In a sentence he'd prepared in German, he asked at the desk that a note he had written in English should be taken to Herr Mayakovsky. The fat, bald-headed manager, or perhaps owner, took it without comment and disappeared up the stairs.

Simeon, as was his habit, spent the time of waiting in vivid imaginings of possible outcomes.

A. A swift return of *le Patron,* or rather, *Mein Wirt,* with a brusque intimation that the distinguished Russian gentleman did not receive every Tom, Dick and Harry who happened to be at a loose end.

B. A message that Simeon should return the next day, or the one after, which would mean kicking his heels around Berlin while the money entrusted to him for a quite different purpose dwindled.

C. A request that he ascend to Mayakovsky's apartment without a moment's delay.

As always, none of these forecasts were fulfilled.

Instead, a pale, dark girl with glowing eyes (years later Simeon recalled these eyes when coming on a book of verse by her second husband, Louis Aragon, called 'Les Yeux d'Elsa') came down to meet him.

She greeted him in almost perfect English and began chatting away as if they knew each other quite well and that this was a friendly call on her. When Simeon at last put a tentative question as to whether Maykovsky was staying at the hotel, she said:— 'Volodya? Oh, he's deep in a poker session that's been going on since early morning for high stakes.

– When is it likely to end?

– There's no telling. Since he arrived here a week ago he's seen nothing of Berlin. He spends all day and half the night playing cards up in his bedroom with some Moscow friends.

Simeon made no direct comment but asked Elsa how she spent her time.

– Oh, we shop, Lili and I. You've no idea if you've only just arrived of what can be bought here for almost nothing because of the inflation. You'll no doubt be fitting yourself out in style.

Little she knew the pangs of guilt that he already was feeling on leaving the Republicans at home in the lurch, as it was, without finally destroying all possibility of excuse on his return by buying suits (did she notice the frayed cuffs of his jacket?) and whatever took his fancy in this city where he should never have been in the first place!

Elsa chatted away, mentioning by Christian name members of the entourage whose relationship he couldn't sort out.

What about seeing how the card-game was progressing, he hesitantly suggested.

She returned after some delay, which Simeon had taken as a hopeful sign, wearing a fur coat that she told him she and Lili had picked up for the equivalent of one dollar.

No news from the Poker session?

– Oh yes, Volodya asks you to meet him tomorrow in the *Romanisches Café* at six o'clock.

Another whole day wasted and the supply of small arms to be delivered to the hard-pressed Republicans dwindling by the hour!

He found a room in a hotel, went to bed early, spent the next morning at the zoological gardens, had a frugal midday meal of Bockwurst and potato salad, and arrived at the rendezvous, situated where the city's principal thoroughfares meet at the *Gedächtnis Kirke*, outside which two tall, late sunflowers were still in bloom, at five minutes past the appointed hour.

Once through the revolving door, the first person he caught sight of was Elsa, still in her fur coat although the heating seemed more than adequate.

Could the tall young man with the cropped head of a convict and the rather scowling expression be Mayakovsky? Yes, it was, and hardly had Elsa introduced them than Simeon was in his bear-like embrace. There was also Lili Brik, the poet's beloved, as she had explained at the hotel, and Osya, Lili's bald husband, as well as Ilya Ehrenberg.

Released, Simeon sat on a chair between Mayakovsky and Elsa and with an expansive, clumsy gesture the poet beckoned a waiter and growled out an order for two bottles of champagne.

After all this it seemed to Simeon an anti-climax to come out with his prepared speech of fraternal greetings, etc., instead of which, with Elsa as interpreter, he managed impromptu, an expression of homage to this man whose poems (the few he had come across) had lit for him some very dark days.

Having seen and spoken with his Russian hero, Simeon decided to return to Brussels by the train that he'd found out left that night. The next morning in Ghent at the dealer's to whom he had the written introduction he'd buy whatever guns what remained of the money allowed, and make for home with the one sparsely filled case.

He played with the notion of a tale about being forewarned of a search of luggage at the Liverpool boat and his being forced to discard most of the weapons, salvaging only what he could dispose about his person. However, to give him his due, he never seriously entertained the idea.

Mayakovsky had his own ideas (about Simeon's early departure) and with an unexpected old-fashioned formality invited him to dinner at Stöcklers.

— Just the two of us, old soldier, with Elsa (who was translating the words) who is angry with me just now, as go-between. And, of course, my sweetest Lissik; possibly Shklovsky too.

Who these last two were Simeon had no idea until Elsa told him that Lissik was one of the endless variations Mayakovsky liked to play on her sister's name. Victor Shklovsky was a Russian emigré living in Berlin.

In the end, Simeon confided in Mayakovsky, whom, like the others, he was now calling Volodya, the true state of his affairs.

The big poet clapped a hand to his brow.

— I guessed there were complications from your worried air the moment I laid eyes on you. God preserve us, you're living under pressures as great as my own! Your beleaguered comrades will not be exposed to the common enemy while we celebrate our happy meeting! You will catch the early morning express with enough good Soviet roubles, which you can change legally in Belgium, to purchase all the guns originally on your list, and one word of advice from a seasoned campaigner: don't neglect to add a few mausers, invaluable in a tight corner, I assure you.

Simeon dined with Vladimir Mayakovsky and a half-dozen others in a fashionable restaurant on Kurfurstendamm on a mild October night in 1922, on turtle soup, langoustine and raspberry compote, a bundle of paper roubles, engraved with Lenin's head, stowed away in his pocket, drinking French wine, his host disdaining Rhine and Moselle.

from

Autumn Sunshine

a story

THE RECTORY WAS IN CO. WEXFORD, eight miles from Enniscorthy.
It was a handsome eighteenth century house, with Virginia
creeper covering three sides and a tangled garden full of
quince and struggling japonica which had always been too much
for its incumbents. It stood alone, seeming lonely even,
approximately at the centre of the country parish it served. Its
church – St Michael's Church of Ireland – was two miles away, in
the village of Boharbawn.

For twenty-six years the Morans had lived there, not wishing
to live anywhere else. Canon Moran had never been an ambitious
man; his wife, Frances, had found contentment easy to attain in
her lifetime. Their four girls had been born in the rectory, and had
become a happy family there. They were grown up now, Frances's
death was still recent: like the rectory itself, its remaining
occupant was alone in the countryside. The death had occurred in
the spring of the year, and the summer had somehow been
bearable. The clergyman's eldest daughter had spent May and part
of June at the rectory with her children. Another one had brought
her family for most of August, and a third was to bring her newly
married husband in the winter. At Christmas nearly all of them
would gather at the rectory and some would come at Easter. But
that September, as the days drew in, the season was melancholy.

Then, one Tuesday morning, Slattery brought a letter from
Canon Moran's youngest daughter. There were two other letters as
well, in unsealed buff envelopes which meant that they were
either bills or receipts. Canon Moran had been wondering if he
should give the lawn in front of the house a last cut when he

heard the approach of Slattery's van. The lawnmower was the kind that had to be pushed, and in the spring the job was always easier if the grass had been cropped close at the end of the previous summer. He was frail and grey-haired in his elderliness and always wore the clothes of his calling.

"Isn't that a great bit of weather, Canon?" Slattery remarked, winding down the window of the van and passed out the three envelopes. "We're set for a while, would you say?"

"I hope so, certainly."

"Ah, we surely are, sir."

The conversation continued for a few moments longer, as it did whenever Slattery came to the rectory. The postman was young and easy-going, not long the successor to old Mr. O'Brien, who'd been making the round on a bicycle when the Morans first came to the rectory in 1952. Mr O'Brien used to talk about his garden, Slattery talked about fishing and often bought a share of his catch to the rectory.

"It's a great time of year for it," he said now, "except for the darkness coming in."

Canon Moran smiled and nodded, the van turned round on the gravel, dust rising behind it as it moved swiftly down the avenue to the road. Everyone said Slattery drove too fast.

He carried the letters to a wooden seat on the edge of the lawn he'd been wondering about cutting. Deirdre's handwriting hadn't changed since she'd been a child; it was round and neat, not at all a reflection of the girl she was. The blue English stamp, the Queen in profile blotched a bit by the London postmark, wasn't on its side or half upside down, as you might possibly expect with Deirdre. Of all the Moran children, she'd grown up to be the only difficult one. She hadn't come to the funeral and hadn't written about her mother's death. She hadn't been to the rectory for three years.

I'm sorry, she wrote now. *I couldn't stop crying actually. I've never known anyone as nice or as generous as she was. For ages I didn't even want to believe she was dead. I went on imagining her in the rectory and doing the flowers in church and shopping in Enniscorthy.*

Deirdre was twenty-one now. He and Frances had hoped she'd go to Trinity and settle down, but although at school she'd seemed to be the cleverest of their children she'd had no desire to become a student. She'd taken the Rosslare boat to Fishguard one night, having said she was going to spend a week with her friend Maeve Coles in Cork. They hadn't known she'd gone to England until they received a picture postcard from London telling them not to worry, saying she'd found work in an egg-packing factory.

Well I'm coming back for a little while now, she wrote, if you could put up with me and if you wouldn't find it too much. I'll cross over to Rosslare on the 29th, the morning crossing, and then I'll come on to Enniscorthy on the bus. I don't know what time it will be but there's a pub just by where the bus drops you so could we meet in the small bar there at six o'clock and then I won't have to lug my cases too far? I hope you won't mind going into such a place. If you can't make it or don't want to see me it's understandable, so if you don't turn up by half six I'll see if I can get a bus on up to Dublin. Only I need to get back to Ireland for a while.

It was, as he and Slattery had agreed, a lovely autumn. Gentle sunshine mellowed the old garden, casting an extra sheen of gold on leaves that were gold already. Roses that had been ebullient in June and July bloomed modestly now, Michaelmas daisies were just beginning to bud. Already the crab-apples were falling, buddleia had a forgotten look. Canon Moran carried the letter from his daughter into the walled vegetable garden and leant against the side of a greenhouse, half sitting on a protruding ledge, reading the letter again. Panes of glass were broken in the greenhouse, white paint and putty needed to be renewed, but inside a vine still thrived, and was heavy now with black, ripe fruit. Later that morning he would pick some and drive into Enniscorthy, to sell the grapes to Mrs Roche in Slaney Street.

Love, Deirdre: the letter was marvellous. Beyond the rectory the fields of wheat had been harvested, and the remaining stubble had the same tinge of gold in the autumn light; the beech trees and the chestnuts were triumphantly magnificent. But decay and rotting were only weeks away, and the letter from Deirdre was full of life. Love, Deirdre were words more beautiful than all the season's glories. He prayed as he leant against the sunny greenhouse, thanking God for this salvation.

For all the years of their marriage Frances had been a help. As a younger man, Canon Moran often hadn't known quite what to do. He'd been at a loss among his parishioners, hesitating in the face of this weakness or that: the pregnancy of Alice Pratt in 1953, the argument about grazing rights between Mr Willoughby and Eugene Ryan in 1960, the theft of an altar cloth from St Michael's and reports that Mrs Tobin had been seen wearing it as a skirt. Alice Pratt had been going out with a Catholic boy, one of Father

Hayes's flock, which made the matter more difficult than ever. Eugene Ryan was one of Father Hayes's also, and so was Mrs Tobin.

"Father Hayes and I had a chat," Frances had said, and she'd had a chat as well with Alice Pratt's mother. A month later Alice Pratt married the Catholic boy, but to this day attended St Michael's every Sunday, the children going to Father Hayes. Mrs Tobin was given Hail Marys to say by the priest; Mr Willoughby agreed that his father had years ago granted Eugene Ryan the grazing rights. Everything, in these cases and in many others, had come out all right in the end: order emerged from the confusion that Canon Moran so disliked, and it was Frances who always began the process. No one ever said in the rectory that she understood the mystery of people as well as he understood the teachings of the New Testament. She'd been a freckled-faced girl when he'd married her, pretty in her way. He was the one with the brains. Frances saw human frailty everywhere: it was weakness in people, she said, that made them what they were as much as strength did. And she herself had her own share of such frailty, falling short in all sorts of ways of the God's image her husband preached about. With the small amount of housekeeping money she could be allowed she was a spendthrift, and she said she was lazy. She loved clothes and often overreached herself on visits to Dublin. She sat in the sun while the rectory gathered dust and the garden became rank. It was only where people were concerned that she was practical. But for what she was her husband had loved her with unobtrusive passion for seventeen years, appreciating her conversation and the help she'd given him because she could so easily sense the truth. When he'd found her dead in the garden one morning he'd felt he had lost some part of himself.

Though many months had passed since then, the trouble was that Frances hadn't yet become a ghost. Her being alive was still too recent, the shock of her death too raw. He couldn't distance himself, the past refused to be the past. Often he thought that her fingerprints were still in the rectory, and when he picked the grapes or cut the grass of the lawn it was impossible not to pause and remember other years. Autumn had been her favourite time.

Notes on the Writers

JOHN BANVILLE was born in Wexford town in 1945. He now lives in Dublin and is a journalist with *The Irish Press*. His first novel, *Long Lankin* (Secker & Warburg, 1970), was followed a year later by *Nightspawn* (Secker & Warburg, 1971). His third novel, *Birchwood* (Secker & Warburg, 1973), won the Allied Irish Banks prize. John Banville also received a Macaulay fellowship and the American-Irish Foundation literary award. His most recent novel *Doctor Copernicus* (Secker & Warburg, 1976) is to be followed in 1980 by *Kepler*.

SAMUEL BECKETT was born in Dublin in 1906 and studied French and Italian at Trinity College, Dublin. From 1928 to 1930 he taught at the Ecole Normale Superieure, Paris, and then became a lecturer in French at TCD (1930-32). He then resigned his post and spent the next four years in France, Germany and London, finally settling in Paris in 1936, where he has been living since. Of his numerous plays, poems, translations and novels, written largely in both English and French. the best-known are the trilogy *Molloy, Malone Dies, · The Unnameable* (1950), *Waiting for Godot* (1952), and *Endgame* (1957). He was awarded the Nobel Prize for Literature in 1969.

EAVAN BOLAND was born in Dublin in 1944, the daughter of a diplomat. She was educated in London, New York, Dublin, and studied at Trinity College, Dublin. There she took a first in English and lectured for a period. She lives in Dublin and has contributed regularly to *The Irish Times* for a number of years. She collaborated with Micheál Mac Liammóir in writing *W. B. Yeats and His World* (Thames & Hudson 1971). Her poems have been published in *The Dublin Magazine, The Irish Times* and *Harper's Bazaar*; they have been recorded for Harvard. In 1968 she was awarded a Macaulay fellowship for poetry. Her first collection, *New Territory* (Figgis, 1967), was followed by *The Warhorse* (Victor Gollancz) in 1975. She and her husband, the novelist Kevin Casey, are currently Fellows at the Iowa International Writing Programme. A new book, *In Her Own Image,* will be published by Arlen House this spring.

EILÉAN NÍ CHUILLEANÁIN, born in 1942 in Cork, was educated at University College, Cork, and at Oxford. She has been a lecturer in English at Trinity College, Dublin, since 1966 and an editor of *Cyphers* since its foundation in 1975. She is married to another editor and poet, Macdara Woods. In 1966 she received the Irish Times award for poetry, followed by the Patrick Kavanagh award for her first collection *Acts and Monuments* (Gallery Books, 1972). Since then she has published two further collections, *Site of Ambush* (Gallery Books, 1975) and *The Second Voyage* (Gallery Books, 1977). She has also brought out a book, *Cork* (Gallery Books, 1977), in collaboration with the artist Brian Lalor.

SEAMUS DEANE, born in Derry 1940, was educated at St. Columb's, Derry, Queen's University Belfast and later at Cambridge where he took his Ph.D. The years 1966-68 he spent at American universities and since 1969 has been lecturer in English at University College, Dublin. In 1977-78 he was visiting lecturer at the University of Indiana, Notre Dame and Berkeley. He has published many articles in scholarly journals such as *La Revue de Littérature Comparée, Modern Language Review, Journal of the History of Ideas.* Former editor of *Atlantis* (1969-73), he is currently guest editor of the *Crane Bag.* Apart from the many poems published in journals and anthologies, Seamus Deane has published two collections, *Gradual Wars* (Irish University Press, 1972), which won the A.E. literary award, and *Rumours* (Dolmen Press, 1979).

PAUL DURCAN has lived in Cork for the past eight years as a full-time writer. Born in Dublin 1944, he took his degree in Archaeology and Mediaeval History at University College, Cork. He collaborated with Brian Lynch on his first book, *Endsville* (New Writer's Press, 1967); in 1969 he recorded poems for Harvard University and the British Arts Council, and founded with Martin Green the biquarterly *Two Rivers* which ran for two years. He won the Patrick Kavanagh Award in 1974 and followed this by his first solo collection, *O Westport in the Light of Asia Minor* (Anna Livia Books, Dublin Magazine Press, 1975). Since then, he has published two further collections, *Teresa's Bar* (Gallery Books, 1976) and *Sam's Cross* (Profile Poetry, 1978). His poetry has also been published in anthologies, such as *Poetry Now I* (Goldsmith Press, 1975) and *The Wearing of the Black* (ed. P. Fiacc, Blackstaff Press 1974), and in magazines such as *Magill, Choice, Cyphers.* He has been writing a weekly column for the *Cork Examiner* since 1977 and is editor of the new arts magazine *The Cork Review.*

PETER FALLON was born in 1951 and grew up on a farm in Co. Meath. In 1970 he founded the Gallery Press and he continues to edit and publish poems, plays and stories by Irish authors. He has published booklets in Ireland and America and three collections of his own poems in Dublin, *Co-incidence of Flesh* (1972), *The First Affair* (1974) and *The Speaking Stones* (1978). He has toured America four times giving readings and lectures and was poet-in-residence at Deerfield Academy in Massachusetts in 1976-77. He edited *The Second Voyage* (Wake Forest U. Press, 1977) and is co-editor of Deerfield Press books, of *The First Ten*

Years (Dublin Arts Festival Poetry, 1979) and *Soft Day: a miscellany of contemporary Irish writing* (U. of Notre Dame Press, 1979/Wolfhound, 1980). He is currently editing a selection from *The Bell 1940-54* for the O'Brien Press. He lives in Loughcrew in North Meath, helping on a sheep farm, cutting wood.

BRIAN FRIEL was born in Co. Tyrone in 1929 and now lives in Donegal. Educated at St. Columb's, Derry, Maynooth College, and St. Joseph's Teachers' Training College, Belfast, he worked as a schoolteacher from 1956 until 1960, when he became a full-time writer. A winner of the Macauley Fellowship, he was appointed shareholder of the Abbey Theatre in 1965. Apart from his many plays, produced on radio, on television and on the stage, Brian Friel has also written short stories, mainly for the *New Yorker*, which were collected in *The Saucer of Larks* (Victor Gollancz, 1962) and *The Gold in the Sea* (Victor Gollancz, 1966). His plays include *Philadelphia Here I Come* (Faber & Faber, 1965), *The Loves of Cass Maguire* (Faber and Faber, 1967), *Crystal and Fox* (Faber and Faber, 1970), *Freedom of the City* (Faber and Faber, 1974), *Living Quarters* (Faber and Faber, 1978), *Volunteers* (Faber and Faber, 1979) and, more recently, *Aristocrats* and *Faith Healer*. The Gallery Press published *The Enemy Within* and *Selected Stories* in 1979.

MICHAEL HARTNETT, born in Co. Limerick in 1941, came to Dublin in 1963 and was co-editor of *Arena* until 1965. Since then, he has held a variety of jobs in Dublin and London, including those of poetry critic of *The Irish Times*, co-editor of *Choice* (Goldsmith Press, 1973), postman and housepainter. He has returned to live in Co. Limerick and to write in Irish. His first collection of poems, *Anatomy of a Cliché* (Dolmen Press, 1968) was followed in 1970 by *Selected Poems of Michael Hartnett* (New Writers' Press, 1970). He has also published *Tao: a Version of the Chinese Classic of the Sixth Century* (New Writers' Press, 1971) and *Gypsy Ballads: a Version of the 'Romancero Gilato'* (Goldsmith Press, 1973). In 1975 he decided to write solely in Irish and so published *A Farewell to English* (Gallery Books, 1975, enlarged edition, 1978); this won the Irish-American Culture award and an Arts Council award, and was followed by *Poems in English* (Dolmen Press, 1977). His first collection in Irish, *Adharca Broic* (Gallery Books, 1978) is to be followed shortly by another.

SEAMUS HEANEY has won many awards for his poetry, including the Eric Gregory award (1967), the Irish-American Cultural Foundation award (1972) and the Duff Cooper Memorial (1975). Born in Derry in 1939, he was educated at St. Columb's, Derry, and at Queen's University, Belfast. He taught for a year in a secondary school before becoming a lecturer at St. Joseph's College of Education, Belfast (1963-66). From 1968 until 1972 he was a lecturer at QUB and spent a year as a guest lecturer at Berkeley. In 1972 he moved to Co. Wicklow to take up writing full-time and in 1975 was appointed lecturer at Carysfort College, Dublin, a post he still holds; he moved to Dublin in 1976. He edited *Soundings* (Blackstaff Press) in 1972. His collections of poetry since *Death of a Naturalist* (Faber & Faber, 1966) have been *Door into the Dark* (Faber & Faber, 1969), *Wintering Out* (Faber & Faber, 1972), *North* (Faber & Faber, 1975) and *Field Work* (Faber & Faber, 1979).

JOHN HEWITT, born in 1907 in Belfast, and educated at the Methodist College and Queen's University, Belfast, is a fellow of the Museums Association, a member of the Irish Academy of Letters since 1960, and an hon. D.Litt. of the New University of Ulster, Coleraine. His professional career was spent in the Belfast Museum and Art Gallery (1930-57) and in the Herbert Art Gallery and Museum, Coventry, where he was Art Director. Apart from his contributions to personal journals, he has also been art critic for the *Belfast Telegraph, The Irish Times* and the *Birmingham Post*. His poetry was first printed in short-lived periodicals in the late 'twenties and has been represented since in various anthologies. Since 1976 he has been poet-in-residence at QUB where he prepared his most recent collection, *The Rain Dance* (Blackstaff Press, 1978). His other collections include *No Rebel Word* (F. Muller, 1948), *Collected Poems 1932-67* (McGibbon & Kee, 1968), *Out of my Time* (Blackstaff Press, 1974) and *Time Enough* (Blackstaff Press, 1976).

AIDAN HIGGINS was born in Celbridge, Co. Kildare, in 1927 and educated at Clongowes Wood College. He has subsequently worked in England and South Africa, and since 1962 has been living in London and the South of Spain. His first volume of short stories, *Felo De Se* (Calder, 1960, republished as *Asylum and Other Stories,* John Calder, 1978), was translated into several languages, including Finnish and Rumanian. Higgins was awarded the James Tate Black memorial prize, the Academy of Letters award, and the Berlin residential scholarship. His first novel, *Langrishe Go Down* (Calder & Boyars, 1966) was followed by *Balcony of Europe* (Calder & Boyars, 1972) and *Scenes From a Receding Past* (John Calder, 1977). He has also edited *A Century of Short Stories* (Jonathan Cape, 1977).

DENIS JOHNSTON, born in Dublin in 1901, was educated at Cambridge where he read history and law. After a year at the Law School of Harvard he was called to the English bar (1925) and to the bar of Northern Ireland (1926). Between 1925 and 1929 he was a member of the Dublin Drama League and the New Players; he was director of the Gate Theatre between 1931 and 1936. Giving up his law practice in 1936, he joined the BBC in Belfast, later in London. From 1942-45 he was war correspondent in the Middle East and Europe and was awarded an O.B.E., becoming director of BBC programmes 1946-47. Between 1950 and 1973, the year of his final return to Ireland, he taught at different American universities and there completed his biography of Swift (Hodges Figgis, 1959). Throughout this period he wrote many plays which include *The Moon on the Yellow River* (Jonathan Cape, 1932) *The Old Lady Says No* (Macmillan, 1936), *The Golden Cuckoo and Other Plays* (Jonathan Cape, 1954). In 1977 and 1978 were published the two volumes of his *Dramatic Works* (Colin Smythe), which contain eleven of his plays – some previously unpublished.

JENNIFER JOHNSTON was born in Dublin in 1930, the daughter of the playwright Denis Johnston, and attended schools in Dublin and later Trinity College. She is the author of five novels, *The Captains and the Kings* (Hamish Hamilton, 1972), *The Gates* (Hamish Hamilton, 1973), *How Many Miles to Babylon* (Hamish Hamilton, 1974), *Shadows on our Skin* (Hamish Hamilton, 1977) and *The Old Jest* (Hamish Hamilton, 1979). *Shadows on our Skin* is at present being made into a film by BBC. Her first play, *The Nightingale and not the Lark,* was first presented during the Dublin Theatre Festival, 1979; she is at present working on her second full-length play. Jennifer Johnston is the mother of four children and lives in Derry.

NEIL JORDAN, born in Sligo in 1950, was educated at St. Paul's College, Raheny and at University College, Dublin. He worked with the Children's Theatre Company and on other productions in the city, at the same time publishing stories in "New Irish Writing" (The Irish Press), Stand, London Magazine, Journal of Irish Literature. He has been represented in Best Irish Short Stories (ed. D. Marcus, Elek 1976) and in Paddy No More (ed. William Vorm, Wolfhound Press, 1978). His first collection of short stories, Night in Tunisia (The Irish Writers' Co-operative, 1976), earned him an Arts Council bursary and the Guardian Fiction Prize, for the English edition of the book (published by the Readers and Writers Co-op in 1979). He is currently writing a novel to be published by Jonathan Cape and is involved in the production of a film, Travellers, for which he wrote the script. His play for television, Miracles and Miss Langan, was shown on RTE in November 1979.

BRENDAN KENNELLY is Professor of Modern English Literature at Trinity College, Dublin. Born in Co. Kerry in 1936, and educated at TCD and at Leeds, he became a lecturer at TCD in 1963. He is editor of the Penguin Book of Irish Verse (Penguin Books, 1970). He has given poetry readings in Sweden, Poland, Belgium, England and America, where he has also been visiting professor at Barnard College, New York, and Swarthmore College, Pennsylvania. A recording of his reading is to be brought out in 1980. Since his first books of poems written in collaboration with Rudi Holzapfel – Cast a Cold Eye (Dolmen Press, 1959), The Rain the Moon (Dolmen Press, 1961) – Brendan Kennelly has published over twenty volumes of poetry, including Love Cry (Allen Figgis, 1972), New and Selected Poems (Gallery Books, 1976), Islandman (Profile Press, 1977) and A Small Light (Gallery Books, 1979).

BENEDICT KIELY, born in Co. Tyrone in 1919, was educated locally and took his degree in English at University College, Dublin. He spent most of his life in Dublin, working as a columnist, critic, feature and leader writer, and was literary editor of The Irish Press for several years. He also lectured for a time at UCD as well as at several universities in the U.S., and is a council member of the Irish Academy of Letters. His stories appeared mostly in the New Yorker, but he has also published in the Kilkenny Magazine, Irish Writing, Harper's Bazaar, The Bell and The Irish Bookman. Between 1946 and 1977 he published ten novels including In a Harbour Green (Jonathan Cape, 1949), Honey Seems Bitter (Methuen, 1954), Dogs Enjoy the Morning (Victor Gollancz, 1968) and Proxopera (Victor Gollancz, 1977). He has also published some collections of short stories, e.g. A Journey to the Seven Streams (Methuen 1963, Poolbeg Press, 1977) and A Cow in the House and Other Stories (Victor Gollancz, 1978). Also a non-fiction writer, he has written a biography of William Carleton, Poor Scholar (Sheed & Ward, 1947), Modern Irish Fiction (Golden Eagle Books, 1950) and a book of reminiscences, All the Way to Bantry Bay (Victor Gollancz, 1978).

THOMAS KILROY, born in 1934 in Co. Kilkenny, studied at University College, Dublin, where he took his M.A. From 1959 to 1964 he was headmaster of a Dublin school and spent two years as a visiting lecturer at American universities. In 1965 he was appointed lecturer at UCD, a post he held until in 1972 he decided to devote himself full-time to writing. The years 1975-78 he spent successively at University College, Galway, New Hampshire and UCD until his appointment in 1978 to the chair of English at UCG. He has published a number of articles on Irish dramatists in journals and books such as *J. M. Synge Centenary Papers* (ed. M. Harmon, Dolmen Press, 1972), and edited a full-length study of Seán O'Casey (Twentieth Century Views series, Prentice Hall, 1975). He has published one novel, *The Big Chapel* (Faber & Faber, 1971), but so far he has been primarily a playwright, his plays having been produced on stage, on radio and on television in Dublin, London and several European countries. His first play *The Door* (1967), which was a BBC award winner, was followed by *The Death and Resurrection of Mr. Roche* (Faber & Faber, 1968), first performed at the Dublin Theatre Festival and later taken on tour to England, Holland, Belgium and Germany. *The O'Neill* was first performed at the Peacock Theatre, Dublin, (1969) and was followed in the Abbey Theatre by *Tea & Sex & Shakespeare* in 1976, and by *Talbot's Box* (Gallery Books, 1979), first performed at the Abbey in 1977 and subsequently taken to London.

THOMAS KINSELLA, born in Dublin 1928, was educated locally and then entered the Civil Service where he remained for nineteen years. In 1962 he won an Arts Council award for the American edition of his poems and translations. In 1965 he won the Denis Devlin memorial prize which was followed by the position of poet-in-residence at Carbondale (Illinois), where he remained for three years before becoming Professor of English at Temple College, Philadelphia, a post he still retains, although he lives in Dublin for a large part of the year. In 1972 he founded the *Peppercanister* press for the publication of his own work. His translations from the Old Irish culminated in 1970 with the publication of *The Táin* (Dolmen Press, 1970). Since *Another September* (Dolmen Press, 1958), Kinsella has published many volumes of poetry, including: *Downstream* (Dolmen Press, 1962), *Nightwalker* (Dolmen Press, 1967), *Notes from the Land of the Dead* (Cuala Press, 1972), *New Poems* (Dolmen Press, 1973), *One* (Peppercanister, 1974) and *Son of the Night* (Peppercanister, 1978).

MARY LAVIN, former president of the Irish Academy of Letters (1972-74), was born in Massachusetts in 1912 and returned to Ireland at the age of 10. She was educated at University College, Dublin. Initially encouraged to write by Lord Dunsany, who wrote the foreword to her first book, she published her first collection of short stories, *Tales from Bective Bridge* (Michael Joseph, 1943, Poolbeg Press, 1978) in 1943 and was made an hon. D.Litt. of the National University of Ireland in 1968. Apart from her many collections of short stories, she has published two novels, *Mary O'Grady* (Michael Joseph, 1950) and *The House in Clewe Street* (Michael Joseph, 1945). Her stories have been collected in *The Stories of Mary Lavin* (Constable, 1964); original titles include *The Long Ago* (Michael Joseph, 1944), *The Becker Wives* (Michael Joseph, 1946), *Patriot Son* (Michael Joseph, 1951) and *The Great Wave* (Macmillan 1961, awarded the Katherine Mansfield prize). Her most recent collection, *The Shrine* (Constable, 1977) was preceded in 1972 by *A Memory* (Constable, 1972). Mary Lavin lives in Dublin and on her farm in Co. Meath.

MICHAEL LONGLEY is Assistant Director of the Arts Council in Belfast and has edited *Causeway: The Arts in Ulster* (Arts Council of Northern Ireland, 1971) and *Under the Moon, Over the Stars* (Arts Council of Northern Ireland, 1971), an anthology of children's verse. Born in Belfast in 1939, he was educated at the Royal Belfast

Academical Institution and at Trinity College, Dublin, where he took a degree in Classics. Formerly poetry critic of *The Irish Times*, his own work has appeared in *The Listener, The New Statesman* and other British and Irish periodicals; it has also been broadcast by the BBC. In 1965, he shared the Gregory award with Derek Mahon. His collections include: *No Continuing City* (Macmillan, 1969), *An Exploded View* (Victor Gollancz, 1973), *Man Lying on a Wall* (Victor Gollancz, 1976) and *The Echo Gate* (Secker and Warburg, 1979), a Poetry Society Choice.

THOMAS McCARTHY was born in Co. Waterford in 1954 and educated at University College, Cork, where he was a founder of the Poetry Workshop later directed by John Montague. He now works at the City Library, Cork. In 1977 he won the Patrick Kavanagh award and in 1978 an Arts Council bursary. He was also a Fellow of the International Writing programme at Iowa University (1978-79). He has published two pamphlets, *Warm Circle* (Miros Press, 1976) and *Shattered Frost* (Miros Press, 1975), and one collection of poems, *The First Convention* (Dolmen Press; 1978). He is at present preparing a second collection, to be called *The Sorrow-Garden*.

TOMÁS MAC SIOMÓIN has been a lecturer of Biology at the College of Technology, Dublin, since 1973. Born in Dublin, he took his degree in science at UCD and then went to Holland and America for further study, taking his doctorate at Cornell University in 1969. His poems have been published in such Irish language magazines as *Comhar, Feasta, Lug, Innti,* and in *The Lace Curtain*. In 1977 he won an Arts Council award for his first collection of poems, *Damhna agus Dánta Eile* (Sairséal agus Dill, 1974). He is currently preparing two further collections called *Achadh Mhoirnín* (Clódhanna Teoranta, to be published very early in 1980) and *Cré agus Cláirseach* (Clódhanna Teo., to be published slightly later). Also a short story writer, he has won prizes at the Oireachtas festival and has contributed to journals and to the anthology *An Díthreabhach* (Mercier Press, 1978, ed. Eoghan O hAnluain).

AIDAN CARL MATHEWS was born in Dublin in 1956 and educated at Gonzaga College. He took his degree in English at University College, Dublin, where he was a prizewinner of the Literary and Historical Society and auditor of the English Literature Society, 1975-76. He spent two years teaching at Belvedere College, Dublin, (1977-79) before going to Trinity College, Dublin, to read for a Master's degree. In 1974 he won *The Irish Times* award for poetry, followed in 1976 by the Patrick Kavanagh award. He won a Macaulay Fellowship in 1978 for his first collection of poems, *Windfalls* (Dolmen Press, 1979).

JOHN MONTAGUE, editor of the *Faber Book of Irish Verse*, has been a lecturer at University College, Cork, since 1972. Born in Brooklyn 1929, he was brought up on a farm in Co. Tyrone and educated at St. Patrick's, Armagh, at UCD and at Yale (1953-54). Between 1954 and 1972, he lived in the USA. where he lectured and organised poetry workshops; in Dublin, as an editor for Bord Fáilte (1956-60); in Paris, as a correspondent of *The Irish Times* (1961-64) and as lecturer at the University of Vincennes (1969-70). He then returned to live permanently in Ireland and published *The Rough Field* in 1972. He has published a collection of short stories, *Death of a Chieftain* (Macgibbon & Kee, 1964) but is principally known for his collections of poems, which, apart from *The Rough Field*, include *Poisoned Lands* (Macgibbon & Kee, 1961, Dolmen Press, 1978), *A Chosen Light* (Macgibbon

& Kee, 1967)', *A Slow Dance* (Dolmen Press, 1975) and *The Great Cloak* (Dolmen Press, 1978). In 1976 he won the Award of the Irish-American Cultural Foundation and in 1977 the Marten Toonder Award for literature.

JOHN MORROW. born in Belfast in 1930, left school at the age of fourteen and worked in the shipyards. Since then, he has held a variety of jobs and still works and lives in Belfast. He began his career by contributing black-humorous pieces to *The Honest Ulsterman*; he also writes regularly for the BBC Northern Ireland. His work has been represented in several anthologies such as *Paddy No More* (ed. W. Vorm, Wolfhound Press, 1978), *Body and Soul* (ed. D. Marcus, Poolbeg Press, 1979). In 1975 he was awarded a bursary by the Arts Council of Northern Ireland and in 1977 his first novel, *The Confessions of Prionsias O'Toole* (Blackstaff Press, 1977) was published. His most recent work has been a collection of short stories, *Northern Myths* (Blackstaff Press, 1978).

PAUL MULDOON lives in Belfast, where he works as a producer for the BBC. Born in Co. Armagh in 1951, he was educated at Queen's University, Belfast. He has published two collections of poems, *New Weather* (Faber & Faber, 1973) and *Mules* (Faber & Faber, 1977). A third collection, *Why Brownlee Left*, is to be brought out by Faber & Faber in the autumn of 1980.

RICHARD MURPHY has lived since 1961 in the area of Cleggan, Co. Galway, and at one time ran a boating business there. Born at Milford House, Co. Galway, he spent the first eight years of his life in Ceylon. He was educated at home, at various public schools in England and at Oxford. He has had a varied career as reviewer, night watchman on the Erriff River, English teacher on Crete, lecturer at the University of London, and writer-in-residence and lecturer at various American universities. In 1951 he won the A.E. memorial award, in 1962 the Guinness poetry award, and in 1967 and 1976 awards from the Arts Council of Britain. His poetry has been collected in the following volumes: *Archaeology of Love* (Dolmen Press, 1955), *Sailing to an Island* (Faber & Faber, 1964), *The Battle of Aughrim* (Faber & Faber, 1968), *High Island* (Faber & Faber, 1974) and *Selected Poems* (Faber and Faber, 1979).

THOMAS MURPHY. born in Tuam, Co. Galway, in 1935, is a director of the Abbey Theatre since 1973. Having retired from teaching in 1962, he went to England to become a full-time writer. Since 1970 he has lived in Ireland and received the Irish Academy of Letters award in 1972. His ten plays have been produced in Dublin, in England and in the U.S. Among his published plays are *A Crucial Week in the Life of a Grocer's Assistant* (1969, Gallery Books 1978), *The Morning After Optimism* (1971, Mercier Press 1973), *The Sanctuary Lamp* (1976, Poolbeg Press 1976) and *On the Outside, on the Inside* (1974, Gallery Books 1976). He has just completed a new play, *The Blue Macushla*, to be performed in Dublin in the near future.

SEÁN Ó FAOLÁIN is a member of the Irish Academy of Letters, a former director of the Arts Council of Ireland, and former editor of *The Bell* (1940-46). Born in Cork in 1900, he was educated at University College, Cork, and, after his participation in the Civil War on the Republican side, at Harvard. He was a lecturer at Boston College in 1929, and for four years taught in Middlesex, during which time he published his first collection of short stories, *Midsummer Night's Madness* (Jonathan Cape, 1932). Since then, he has published over twenty books including novels, short stories, biography, travel, literary criticism, a play, and his auto-biography *Vive Moi* (Little, Brown & Co., 1964). *The Selected Stories of Seán Ó'Faoláin* (Constable, 1978) was preceded by *Foreign Affairs and Other Stories* (Constable, 1976) and *The Talking Trees* (Little, Brown & Co., 1968, Jonathan Cape, 1971). Other titles include *The Vanishing Hero* (Eyre & Spottiswood, 1956), *The Irish* (Penguin Books, 1947) and *Bird Alone* (Jonathan Cape, 1936). Seán O Faolain now lives in Dublin and has recently published a new novel, *And Again?* (Constable, 1979).

LIAM O'FLAHERTY was born on the Aran Islands in 1896. Educated at the local National School, Rockwell College, Blackrock College and University College, Dublin, he joined the Irish Guards in 1915. He was invalided out of the army in 1917 and was awarded a war degree on his return to Ireland. Having taken some part in the Civil War, he moved to London in 1922 and in the following year published his first novel, *Thy Neighbour's Wife* (Jonathan Cape, 1923). He was a founder member of the Irish Academy of Letters. While returning periodically to Ireland, he has travelled widely: he went to Russia in 1931 and spent the war years in Connecticut, the Caribbean and South America, where he began again to write in Irish, publishing *Dúil* (Sáirseal agus Dill, 1953). In 1956, the collected *Stories of Liam O'Flaherty* (Devin-Adair, 1956) were published. Apart from his several collections of short stories, O'Flaherty has written three autobiographical novels and more than twenty other novels including *Skerrett* (Victor Gollancz, 1932), *Famine* (Victor Gollancz, 1937) and *Insurrection* (Victor Gollancz, 1950). Wolf-hound Press, Dublin, is publishing much of his work. They first published *The Pedlar's Revenge and Other Stories* in 1976 and *The Wilderness* in 1978 and have already re-issued *Skerrett* (1977), *The Test of Courage* (1977), *The Ecstasy of Angus* (1978), *All Things to Come: a Rabbit Story* (1977) and *Famine* (1979).

DESMOND O'GRADY was born in Limerick in 1935 but spent most of his childhood in West Clare and in the Irish-speaking districts of Co. Kerry. After a period in Dublin in the 'fifties he left Ireland for Paris (1955) and Rome (1957-62), where he was assistant headmaster at an English school. He also was European editor of the *Transatlantic Review*. In 1962 he went to Harvard and took his M.A. in Celtic Studies. Since his first collection of poems, *Chords and Orchestrations* (The Echo Press, 1956), he has published many poems and translations leading, in 1977, to his translation of the Middle Welsh poem by Aneirin, *The Gododdin* (Dolmen Press) His versions of Irish, Italian and American poetry were published under the title *Off Licence* (Dolmen Press, 1968). For a number of years, Desmond O'Grady has been poet-in-residence at the American University of Cairo, and although he spends a lot of time in Ireland his permanent home is in Greece. His poetry, which has been translated into many languages, including Arabic, has been published in thirteen books, such as *Reilly* (Phoenix Press, 1961), *Separations* (Goldsmith Press, 1973), *Sing Me Creation* (Gallery Books, 1977), *A Limerick Rake* (Gallery Books, 1978) and *The Headgear of the Tribe*: new and selected poems, edited by Peter Fallon (Gallery Books, 1979) and *His Skaldcrane's Nest* (Gallery Books, 1979).

LIAM Ó MUIRTHILE works as a journalist in RTE. Born in Cork 1950, he went to University College, Cork, where he studied Irish and French and became involved with the group of young poets around the broadsheet/magazine *Innti* (1970-73). He was manager of the Slógadh festival for one year and has published poems in many Irish language magazines, including *Comhar, Feasta, Lug* and *Scríobh*. He is currently preparing a collection to be called *Sa Chaife agus Dánta Eile.*

FRANK ORMSBY has been editor of *The Honest Ulsterman* since 1969. Born in Co. Fermanagh in 1947, he was educated at St. Michael's College, Enniskillen, and at Queen's University, Belfast, where he took his M.A. in English; he has taught at the Royal Belfast Academical Institution since 1971. In 1974 he won the Gregory award for poetry. His poetry has been published in pamphlets such as *Ripe for Company* (Ulsterman Publications, 1971), *Business As Usual* (Ulsterman Publications, 1973) and *Being Walked by a Dog* (Ulsterman Publications, 1979). His most recent work has been the anthology *Poets from the North of Ireland* (Blackstaff Press, 1979), which he has edited. In 1977 he published his first solo collection of poems, *A Store of Candles* (Oxford U.P., 1977), a Poetry Society Choice.

CATHAL Ó SEARCAIGH, born 1956, is a native speaker of Irish from Meenala, Co. Donegal. He was educated at the local national and vocational schools and then at the National Institute for Higher Education, Limerick, where he studied French, Russian and Irish. After working in London for a year he went to Maynooth College in 1977 to do Celtic Studies. Since 1978 he has been working with RTE in the production of the programme in Irish "Aisling Gheal". He has published many poems in Irish language magazines such as *Comhar, Scríobh* and *Feasta,* and with Gabriel Rosenstock and Bill Doyle has brought out *Tuirlingt* (Carabad, 1979). His first solo collection was *Miontragéide Cathrach* (Cló Uí Chuirreáin, 1975) and he is now preparing a second collection, *Scrúda Coinsiasa agus Dánta Eile.*

SEÁN Ó TUAMA, born in Cork in 1926, had a bilingual upbringing in Irish and English and is at present associate professor of Irish language and literature at University College, Cork. He was visiting professor at Harvard (1966), research professor at Jesus College, Oxford (1977) and has lectured extensively in American, English and French universities. His study of the relationship between Irish folksong and medieval French verse was published as *An Grá in Amhráin na nDaoine* (Sáirséal agus Dill, 1960). He has also edited *The Gaelic League Idea* (Mercier Press, 1973), *Caoineadh Airt Uí Laoghaire* (Clóchomhar Teo., 1961), *Nuabhéarsaíocht* (Sáirséal agus Dill, 1950) and a bilingual anthology, *Poems of the Dispossessed,* in collaboration with Thomas Kinsella (to be published shortly by the Dolmen Press). He has written nine plays, including *Gunna Cam agus Sleabhra Óir* (Sáirséal agus Dill, 1967) and *Moloney* (Clóchomhar Teo., 1967). His collections of verse are *Faoileán na Beatha* (Clóchomhar Teo., 1962) and *Saol fó Thoinn* (Clóchomhar Teo., 1978).

MÍCHEÁL Ó SIADHAIL, born in Dublin, was educated at Trinity College, Dublin, where he studied Celtic Languages, and at the University of Oslo, where he studied Scandinavian Languages and Folklore. From 1969 until 1973, when he resigned the post to devote more time to writing, he was a lecturer in Irish at TCD; he subsequently joined the Dublin Institute for Advanced Studies where he still works in the field

A BIBLE STORY

Retold and illustrated by JEAN MARZOLLO

Daniel in the Lions' Den

LITTLE, BROWN AND COMPANY

New York ⌇ An AOL Time Warner Company

Who's that?   That's the angel.   What did the angel do?   You'll find out—but not right away.   First, meet Daniel.

Introduction

Daniel was born in Jerusalem long, long ago. On the map there is a picture of a little boy. That's Daniel in Jerusalem. Jerusalem is where Daniel learned about God. He learned to pray to God every day.

Daniel's people, the Jews, lost a war to the Babylonians. Because they lost, they had to move to Babylon to serve the king who won the war. On the map there's a picture of a man. That's the grown-up Daniel in Babylon.

The Story: Daniel in the Lions' Den

One day in the city of Babylon there was a brand new king. His name was Darius. King Darius picked various Babylonian men to help him rule his kingdom. At first, these men were THRILLED.

Daniel grew up in Babylon. He served the king well and, in time, became a very important man. But Daniel always missed the city he came from. Every day he looked out his window toward Jerusalem and prayed to God, just as he had learned to do when he was a boy.

But then King Darius chose Daniel to be their boss. Now the men were FURIOUS!

NOT FAIR!

Daniel's different. He's a Jew from Jerusalem!

What gives him the right to be the boss of us?

Let's get him into trouble.

For days and weeks, the troublemakers watched Daniel closely, but they never found him doing anything wrong.

He works hard.

He's fair.

The troublemakers went to the king and gave him their BIGGEST smiles.

How can praying get Daniel into trouble? He prays to a different God than the Babylonians. And they don't like that.

The troublemakers watched Daniel's house. The minute they saw him praying, they ran to the king to tattle.

Daniel and the lions slept peacefully all night long. After a while, the angel left to check on the king. King Darius was not in his bed. He felt so bad about Daniel that he couldn't sleep a wink.

You think the angel should help the king sleep?   No way.

Daniel and the angel sang lullabies until the lions fell asleep.

Gentle, lovely, yellow lions,
Now it's time to sleep.
Especially you, Dear Baby Lion,
Remember . . . not a peep!*

*You can sing this to the
tune of "Row, Row, Row
Your Boat."

But Baby Lion roared again. At this point Daniel stepped forward and smiled.

If you don't close your mouth, Baby Lion, you'll get in trouble with the angel. So, here's a question for you: Can you put your big sharp teeth together and say, 'Mmm-hmm?'

Mmm-hmm!

Is Baby Lion in trouble?   No, the angel is happy now *because* Daniel is safe from the lions' sharp teeth.

The father lion and the mother lion closed their mouths immediately. But not the baby lion.

ROAR! ROAR! ROAR!

Look at my BIG teeth!

Let's stop and watch!

Okay, but just for a minute!

What have I done?

He signed a bad law.   He made a huge mistake and he knows it.

Because I did nothing wrong, my God sent an angel, who closed the lions' mouths so they could not harm me! Oh, King, I will always honor you, and I will always honor my God.

Daniel is loyal to both God and the King.   That's hard to do.   But Daniel can do it!

I don't see an angel, my friend, but I believe you, and I shall issue a decree. From now on, everyone in Babylon will respect and honor the God of Daniel, the living God who performs wonders in heaven and on earth!

So King Darius is a good King, after all.   Yes.   What happened to the troublemakers?

Amen!

I'm not sure, but I heard that, by order of the king, the lions had a very tasty breakfast.   Yuck!

What have WE got to eat today?   Honey!   Bread crumbs!

"Look at my wings! Look at my starry wand!" she squeaked, twirling and whirling.

"Now I'm a real, real fairy!" she sang, as she spun and danced.

"You're a fairy princess," smiled Daddy, "and you need an enchanted castle. Come and look . . ."

Phoebe peeped into her bedroom.

"Wow!" she whispered.

Her bedroom sparkled with more birthday presents—new stars and twinkles and silvery sprinkles.

"Make us some magic, Phoebe," said her big brother Sam.

"I'm going to fly first!" said Phoebe.

She raced into the garden and scrambled up onto the old tree stump.

"I will fly just like a fairy," she thought.

She stood on tiptoe and stretched her arms.

She jumped high into the air,
waving her wand . . .

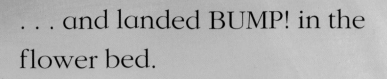

. . . and landed BUMP! in the
flower bed.

"Oh, dear," sighed Phoebe, "maybe flying is too hard for a brand new fairy. I'll practice making wishes instead."

She decided to start with a wish for Sam.

He was playing pirates in the kiddie pool.

"I'm Fairy Fizzwhizz," Phoebe announced.

"Tell me your wish, and I'll make it come true!"

"Go away pesky pixie, or you'll walk the plank!" Sam growled.

"I'm not a pixie!" Phoebe stamped.
"Now make a wish, or I'll bop you!"
"All right," Sam laughed. "I wish
I had a parrot."

Phoebe skipped happily through the garden.
"What shall I use for a parrot?" she wondered . . .

. . . and there, on a leaf, she
spotted a ladybug.
  "Perfect," she thought, and began
her spell.

"Ibb-*bib*-*bob* –
oh, do stay still!

"Tip-*tap*-*top* –
stop flying!

"Oh you mean ladybug, come
back!!!" she shouted, as it
zoomed away.

"I'm not a very good fairy,"
Phoebe sighed to Mommy
and Daddy. "I can't fly, and I
can't make a parrot by magic."

"Never mind," said Daddy.
"We need some magic here.
You can add fairy sprinkles
to the cupcakes for your
birthday party—yummy!"

Phoebe made the cakes look so special,
she felt just like a fairy again.
"I'm going to tell Sam I really
can do magic!" she said.

But oh, dear, poor Sam
was in a tizz. The mast
of his ship had snapped in two.
"It won't mend," he said sadly.
"Now I can't be a pirate anymore."

"Don't worry, I'll fix it!" said Phoebe.
"My magic's getting better.
I just needed practice!"

Phoebe twirled twice, then tapped the mast gently. Nothing happened.

She thought and thought.

"I know," she said. "We'll close our eyes and wish very hard."

Sam closed his eyes, but Phoebe tiptoed to the boat.

"*One . . . two . . . three . . . fiddle-de-dee . . .*" she whispered.

"Ta-daaa!"

Sam opened his eyes . . . and saw a
sparkling new mast on his pirate ship.

"You really can do magic, Fairy
Fizzwhizz!" he laughed.

"I did, I did!" squealed Phoebe, and
they sailed together until Daddy
called, "Ahoy there, party-time!"

Mommy and Daddy, Phoebe and Sam shared a fabulous fairy birthday feast.

"I like being a fairy," yawned Phoebe as the stars began to shine.

"You are a fantastic fairy," said Mommy, "but even birthday fairies need their beds." And she carried Phoebe up to her fairy castle.

As Mommy kissed her good-night,
Phoebe whispered in her ear,
"I didn't really do fairy magic,
Mommy."

"Oh, yes, you did," said Mommy.
"You were kind and thoughtful,
and you helped Sam feel
happy. That's the best fairy
magic in the world."

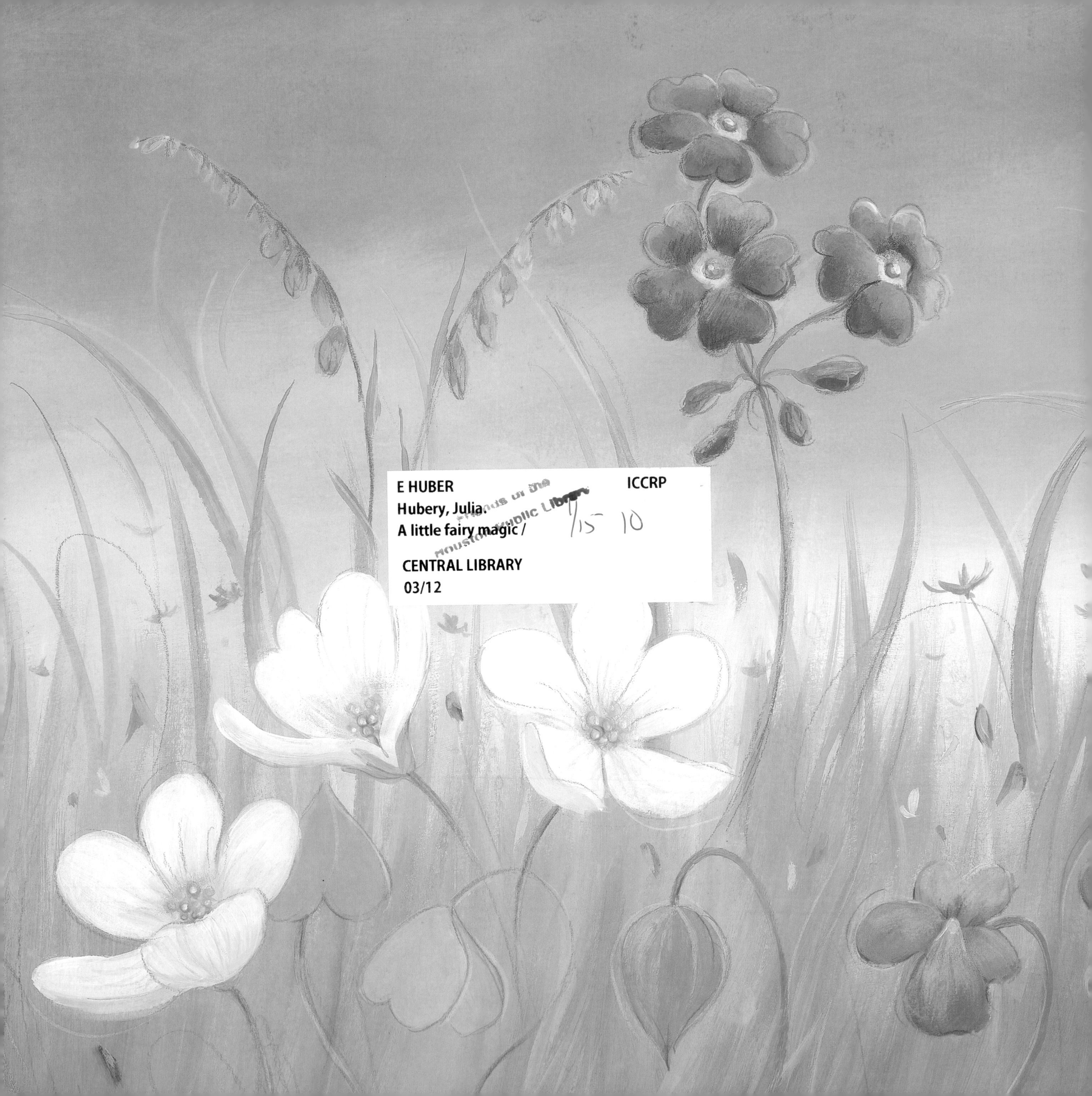